THE GLOBALIZATION
OF BUSINESS
AND THE MIDDLE EAST

THE GLOBALIZATION
OF BUSINESS
AND THE MIDDLE EAST

Opportunities and Constraints

Masoud Kavoossi

Q

QUORUM BOOKS
Westport, Connecticut • London

Library of Congress Cataloging-in-Publication Data

Kavoossi, Masoud.
    The globalization of business and the Middle East : opportunities and
constraints / Masoud Kavoossi.
        p. cm.
    Includes bibliographical references and index.
    ISBN 1–56720–203–9 (alk. paper)
    1. Middle East—Foreign economic relations.   2. Middle East—Economic
conditions—1979–   3. Middle East—Economic integration.   I. Title.
    HF1583.3 .K38   2000
    337.56—dc21   99–056360

British Library Cataloguing in Publication Data is available.

Library of Congress Catalog Card Number: 99–056360
ISBN: 1–56720–203–9

First published in 2000

Quorum Books, 88 Post Road West, Westport, CT 06881
An imprint of Greenwood Publishing Group, Inc.
www.quorumbooks.com

Printed in the United States of America

The paper used in this book complies with the
Permanent Paper Standard issued by the National
Information Standards Organization (Z39.48–1984).

10 9 8 7 6 5 4 3 2 1

To the memory of my mother, Azar, who inspired me to write this book

Contents

Introduction

Events in the last decade have transformed the Middle East: the Iranian revolution, the Iran-Iraq War, the Rushdie affair, the Gulf War. Many countries in the region remain under the threat of international- or U.S.-imposed trade sanctions, including Iran, Iraq, and Libya, as well as Pakistan. The outside world now reaches into the most closed homes, through the various consumer products exported into the region. Processes of modernization, industrialization, and westernization have hit traditional cultures so hard and in such a way that they have raised issues for the peoples and governments alike. Middle Easterners are now faced with these issues and have to formulate responses to them. Matters that in the past might have been ignored must be considered with urgency.

One thing, however, is clear: the internationalization of world markets has applied to the Middle East as well. In the course of the last two decades, international business activities in the region have increased greatly. Moreover, this increase is not limited to any one, specific country. It is not just the more populous and larger countries that have engaged and attracted foreign investors; smaller countries are equally active. The Middle East may not have its own Silicon Valley, but for the most part it is properly poised, with the necessary elements in place, to develop into an industrial region, similar to other developing regions of the world.

With a greater degree of Islam's influence on all facets of life, both in the business environment and daily functions, combined with accelerated industrial modernity, all of the Middle East is undergoing fundamental and rapid change. It is my suspicion that this will be a change for the better.

There are various reasons why this should be so. The availability of a high culture, or great tradition, has many features that make it compatible with the requirements of modern life—individualism and a deep sense of community. The painful choice between modernization and Islam, dwelled upon for many years, seems no longer to be so relevant any more. More and more Middle Easterners appear to believe that to be a Muslim is to be modern, that technology and ideology—Islam—are not contradictory, rather complementary. Foreign investors need to be informed that the primary organizing principle in the region remains Islam and tradition, with its internal tensions and variations. It ought to be also recognized that Islamic societies refuse to become post-Islamic, as the modern West became post-Christian. Islam remains as a system of thought and provides an inner compass to its individual adherents and to society as a whole. Middle Eastern Muslims have resisted pressure to reduce Islam to simply one element of culture, preferring to maintain it as a culture, with all of its attributes, elements, and manifestations, such as economics and worldview. The Middle East can be as important in world commerce, in addition to oil, as it is in world politics.

These would seem to be the kinds of general issues that need to be faced in studying international business in the Middle East. That can only be done by concrete and thorough research and analysis, like that provided by the studies assembled in this book. They have remarkable range and penetration, and they make a significant contribution to the understanding of business, environment, and conditions in this very important part of the world.

Successful international business requires the development and implementation of business strategies responsive to different environments. In the Middle East, the economic, social, and political dimensions differ considerably. Multinational companies must be fully informed and aware of these dimensions and the globalization of the region.

Improving International Competitiveness in the Persian Gulf Region: An Assessment

The Persian Gulf region has a significant level of international commerce and investment, as represented in part by an estimated $120 billion in exports and the presence of nearly 1,200 foreign-affiliate firms, with approximately $29 billion in investments in the region. Recent trends point to increased international investment. The region's major international strengths include oil and natural gas, major international airports, ports along the Persian Gulf, high disposable income per household, an educated labor force, a growing high-technology industrial base, and world-class financial centers. In addition, the region is home to many international and regional organizations. In the aftermath of the Arab-Israeli peace accord, people feel more confident about the stability of the region (see Table 1.1). International weaknesses, however, include a lack of positive image, a serious need for surface transportation improvements, lack of efficient and speedy bureaucracies, a perceived high cost of doing business, inadequacies in the workforce, and the absence of a single entity to promote the region internationally.

Many entities in the world, such as the European Union (EU), the Association of Southeast Asian Nations (ASEAN), and nearby competitors, including India, China, Turkey, and the newly independent states of the former Soviet Union, are in competition with the Persian Gulf states in the global marketplace. At this point there is a need to

Table 1.1 Human Development Index, 1994 Selected Gulf States			
Locality	Real GDP per Capita $ (1991)	Adult Literacy Rate Percent (1992)	Number of Years of Schooling (1992)	Human Development Index* (1992)
Saudi Arabia	10,850	64.1	3.9	0.742
UAE	17,000	65	5.6	0.777
Kuwait	13,126	73.9	5.5	0.809
Bahrain	11,536	79	4.3	0.791
Iran	4,670	56	3.9	0.672
Qatar	14,000	79	5.8	0.795
Iraq	3,500	62.5	5	0.614

*A composite of life expectancy, literacy and schooling, and standard of living, measured by purchasing power.

Source: *Human Development Report*, UN Development Program, New York, June 1994.

make a long-term commitment to increase the region's international competitiveness and to develop an integrated strategy for marketing it more effectively. The emerging realignment of global strategic power through new economic and political blocs may produce a reshaped Europe, possibly including some of the former Soviet republics. A second bloc may be led by Japan; it would be mainly trade based. Members here would come mainly from the Pacific Rim. A third bloc could emerge in the Western Hemisphere, led by the United States and including Canada, Mexico, and perhaps Brazil and Chile. Such a bloc would be primarily trade based, but it could eventually also incorporate many political dimensions. The only remaining region with any political and economic significance would be the Middle East.

In the global configuration now emerging, the United States is no longer perceived as a superpower by many in the Middle East, merely a great power. Having decided that only superpowers count, Middle Easterners, Europeans, Asians, and Latin Americans are forging new economic alliances.

This chapter will offer recommendations to improve the region's international competitiveness, image, visibility, business base, and infrastructure in order to expand its capacity to absorb a variety of imports as well as exports, currently absent.

Theoretical and empirical studies suggest a correlation between increased trade and investment and increased national income. Maizels (1968), Koon (1971), and Tyler (1981), among others, established the relations. The Persian Gulf states under study generally confirm this finding. The countries in the region are essentially mono-product economies attempting to diversify their economic base. The disadvantage of basing economic development on the expansion of a primary-sector industry, such as oil, is the potential instability of primary-product prices. The combination of inelastic demand and inelastic supply conditions that are characteristic of the market of many primary products means that changes in price have little short-term effect on the quantity demanded or supplied. The market adjusts mainly through changes in price; it experiences relatively little change in the quantity traded. The result has been fluctuating oil revenues in the face of unstable prices for this key export commodity (Temple, 1994).

In order to reduce uncertainty and provide greater economic stability, the Gulf countries have attempted to diversify their economies. For this they need foreign investment and technology, subsequently enhancing the countries' ability to attract, absorb, and become globally competitive.

Global competitiveness, here, principally refers to the rapid developments in technology, transport, and information that bring the region to par with the more advanced parts of the world. One consequence of the global competitiveness process is to look at the region not as marginal but as something that concerns the global community. There are some hundred million people living in and around the Persian Gulf, in more than eight countries. Owing to the developments in the region, words such as *fatwa, jihad, ayatollah* are now common in the West. Like much of the rest of the world, the region has long been interconnected through international trade and economic interaction. International competitiveness is not necessarily a wholly novel phenomena, unique to recent decades. As a process it is of considerable historical depth (Ahmed and Donnan, 1994).

Findings of this research may serve as a model for other developing regions in the world. The study will further contribute to the field of international business by evaluating and assessing regional efforts to penetrate international markets successfully. While there exist a number of research studies on other regions, there is a deficiency on the Middle East. This research will utilize sources available from governmental and international organizations.

Expected results include the following general recommendations:

- The private sector needs to become more actively involved in the economic affairs of the region.
- Create a regional international business council.
- Develop a spirit of public and private partnership.
- Improve the region's international infrastructure.
- Foster international awareness of the region as a business center.

REGIONAL GROWTH TRENDS

The Persian Gulf region has a rising level of international activity and is home to a growing number of international companies and investors. At present there are more than 1,200 foreign-affiliate firms in the region, employing over 120,000 people and owning property, plants, and equipment worth approximately $12 billion. Some examples are General Motors, IBM, Toshiba, Sharp, Caterpillar, and Honeywell. Iran, Saudi Arabia, and the United Arab Emirates (UAE), which compose the bulk of the population of the Persian Gulf states, have a rapidly growing export base, as evidenced by a 12 percent increase in exports between 1990 and 1994.

The region's international airports—Tehran International, Dubai, Jeddah, and Riyadh International—experienced more than a 50 percent increase in international air passengers between 1988 and 1994. The number of weekly international flights at Tehran International, Dubai International Airport, and Riyadh International increased by 6.3 percent from 1983 to 1993 (Withiam, 1994). In addition, the number of international markets served by Tehran, Dubai, and Riyadh has increased from twenty-two to 102 destinations in more than fifty-seven countries around the world (*Journal of Commerce*, 1994). Between 1983 and 1993, the region accounted for a 2.1 percent global market share in air passengers, and for 2.3 percent of the world's revenue passenger-kilometers in 1991. In 1992 the port of Sharja in the UAE handled 37,400 ton-equivalent units (TEU), a 146 percent increase over 1991, and about fifty-five thousand TEU in 1993 ("New Services," 1993).

GLOBAL COMPETITION AND THE NEED FOR CHANGE

The Persian Gulf region has neither the competitive international reputation nor the economic-development focus of other competing regions. As such, it is not a priority location choice for American and Western European investors. Countries such as India, Turkey, and Indonesia are in competition with the Persian Gulf region for international trade and investment. These states are not only marketing their countries but working to solve infrastructure problems and building their local executives' capacity to trade internationally. At present the Persian Gulf region is doing very little.

The global economy is becoming more, not less, competitive (Porter, 1986). The region possesses the basic assets and intellectual talents to compete with any region on the globe. However, it must operate, harmonize, and engage its combined resources to move forward in a deliberate effort to improve its international competitiveness (Porter, 1986).

PAST COOPERATIVE EXPERIENCES

Numerous agreements have been signed, resolutions passed, and measures adopted to work toward greater cooperation. Some of the better known include the Gulf Cooperation Council (GCC), the Economic Cooperation Organization (ECO), the Economic and Social Council, the Council of Arab Economic Unity, the Arab Common Market, and the Arab Fund for Economic and Social Development (AFESD), among others. Up to three-hundred bilateral and multilateral agreements have been signed by countries in the region and the broader Middle East including Egypt, Turkey, and Lebanon. Kuwait has three agreements and its own fund for development, the Kuwait Fund for Economic Development (KFED). It is followed by Saudi Arabia, Qatar, and Bahrain, each having signed four agreements. The UAE has signed three.

Improving cooperation in the region should aim at the following objectives:

- Accelerate the process of industrial development by removing trade barriers.
- Create wider cooperation for modernization of industries, perhaps modeled after the European Coal and Steel Community (ECSC) (Weekly and Aggarwal, 1987).
- Coordinate the creation and future expansion of regional industries.
- Create and enforce more comprehensive commercial law, e.g., copyright, and other intellectual-property rights.

A policy based on cooperation is necessary to reduce the shortcomings of market imperfections.

RECOMMENDED INTERNATIONAL MARKETING PLAN

- Marketing publications—prepare an updated international directory.
- Business roundtables and seminars on trade opportunities and international business developments in the area.
- Executive marketing programs focused on attracting foreign investment and promoting export activities.
- Export and trade promotion programs—provide small-business technical assistance and advice for area firms.
- Databases supporting trade and investment programs.

Significant resources must be devoted to international marketing, an important step that is badly needed. This will help close the gap, on the marketing side of the equation, that currently exists between the Persian Gulf and other competing regions. There remains the need to focus on assisting local executives in building their capacities to engage in international trade, through networking and education, and on improving the region's delivery system, by upgrading its infrastructure.

STRENGTHS AND WEAKNESSES

Strengths

A summary of the region's international strengths is as follows:

- Geo-economic location; two-thirds of world oil and gas are located in the region. No other region of the world has such economic significance. Decisions of critical international importance are made in Iran, Saudi Arabia, Iraq, Kuwait, and the UAE. There are compelling reasons for business to establish a presence.
- Availability of major ports and airports.
- Instant recognition of the Persian Gulf worldwide.
- Highest median household disposable income in the developing world.
- A world-class professional and business service sector.

- Home to many international banks.
- Home to the Islamic Development Bank, OPEC, Economic Cooperation Organization (ECO), Organization of Arab Petroleum-Exporting Countries (OAPEC).
- Strategic location, particularly well suited to the European Union, given flight times and time-zone differentials. Multinational corporations positioned in the Persian Gulf are enabled to operate south and west around the Mediterranean Sea, North Africa, and Asia.

Airports

Of particular importance is the region's international transportation sector. The importance of international transportation is reflected in the international airlines serving the region's airports: Aeroflot, Austrian Airlines, Air France, All Nippon Airways (ANA), British Airways, KLM Royal Dutch Airlines, Lufthansa German Airlines, Swissair and Alitalia, among others.

Ports

Another important international strength is the number of ports on the Persian Gulf. Steamship lines from around the world call there, transporting a wide variety of cargos, such as automobiles, farm and construction equipment, steel, coal, grain, and many types of liquid and dry bulk commodities. This diversity helps make the ports of the Gulf among the largest in the region. In 1992, the UAE alone handled foreign commercial imports worth $17 billion ("New Services," 1993). Many of the ports are modern, with state-of-the-art facilities and experienced, skilled labor forces. One of the most modern terminals in the region, Sharjah, features a computerized complex for processing cargo.

Proximity to important populations and industrial centers of the region makes the ports gateways to the Middle East's heartland. The port area is an overnight drive from 35 percent of the region's population.

Weaknesses

The weaknesses of the region can be summarized as follows:

- Lack of positive business image and a general perception of economic mismanagement.

- Inadequate transportation infrastructure.
- Reputation for violence and instability.
- Deficiencies in higher education.
- A general stagnation and economic deterioration since the late 1980s.
- Rapid population growth rate and the ensuing high unemployment rate.

Poor Image

The only clear vision of the region is one of oil. Internationally the Gulf region is viewed as an "oil region," with only a vague understanding of its technology and other industries. There needs to be a clear, new business image of the combined region, blending its manufacturing, high tech/petrochemical, communications, and transportation capabilities.

Transportation

Key segments of the highway system are in need of improvements. Roadways are key to international exports, and access to ports needs to be given special attention. A coordinating commission to address these needs is essential in order to deliver improvements.

Reputation for Violence and Instability

The region has an international reputation for violence and instability, particularly due to the media attention focused on the Arab-Israeli conflict. Apart from the human tragedy resulting from violence, this reputation deters international business from considering the region a good site for expansion or relocation. There exists a persistent lack of political will on the part of the region's countries to agree on and implement cooperation measures.

Deficiencies in Higher Education

While the region has a number of good universities, on balance there is a critical need for improvement in the system. Research and development lags behind that of many other developing regions of the world, such as the Pacific Rim.

General Stagnation

Whereas the region performed relatively well in the 1970s, annual economic growth declined sharply to an average of 1 percent per annum in the 1980s, in spite of good resource endowment. The region is heavily dependent on foreign food imports; nearly half of the food consumed is imported from the OECD countries. In addition, the region's industrial base is essentially petroleum related. Generally, industrial development in the region shows a gradual growth. Nevertheless, the role of manufacturing in the national economy remains limited in comparison to many countries, such as Korea or Indonesia. There exists a high level of dependency on the OECD countries in the areas of trade, capital, and technology. The region relies heavily on foreign patents, technical know-how, and technical management.

Rapid Population Growth

Rapid population growth has complicated the management of the economy and has constrained overall progress. Many countries in the region have an annual population growth rate exceeding 3 percent per annum, with the exception of Iran, which has brought its population growth rate down to about 2.7 percent in recent years. The region doubled its population in the decade of the 1980s.

Linked to population growth and the inadequacy of the economic growth rate is high unemployment. This is especially pronounced in Iran, with an unemployment rate of over 15 percent.

Recommendations on Image and Marketing

There is a need to develop and define a new regional identity. The region needs an organization with a regionwide focus responsible for developing promotional materials and international marketing, while inculcating a new image. Marketing materials must convey a cohesive theme designed to portray the region as an international, business-oriented marketplace. This organization would also provide marketing support and materials to the region's private sector in its individual marketing missions.

There is often only limited coordination of the individual marketing efforts of the region's countries. Better coordination is needed to improve efficiency in regional and local marketing.

Produce Internationally Oriented Publications

A major publication should be produced, focused on an international audience, portraying the economic strengths and business opportunities available in the region. This publication should carry a new image of the region and should be translated into foreign languages. A vision of the region's future and how this vision relates to the major industries needs to be clearly communicated. This should particularly target the Japanese, Europeans, and North Americans.

The region needs to be marketed as an area of manageable size for doing business, and regional coordination of tourism efforts must be encouraged in order to attract international visitors into the region. It would be beneficial for international tourists to remain in the region for longer periods than as only a stopping-off point for other destinations (e.g., Israel). Cooperation between all tourism organizations needs to be initiated, and they should be encouraged to increase international tourism and retain international tourists in the region. At a minimum, each country's office of travel and tourism should display and distribute materials on tourist attractions in the others' areas. Consideration should also be given toward establishing:

- A regionwide information desk at international airports.
- A team of economic development professionals, made available to brief visiting non–Middle Eastern executives or delegates.
- Provide shipping line executives visiting the ports of the UAE, Iran, or Saudi Arabia and airline executives visiting the region's airports with briefings and promotional materials.

CONCLUSION

A poor track record of previous attempts at regional economic cooperation must not keep the region's leaders from innovating new mechanisms and plans to achieve international cooperation and competitiveness. It is not easy to embark on a substantial cooperative effort in a subregion that has suffered its share of mistrust. This is further complicated by the problem of precisely predicting the effects of change in the region's economic and political environment, individual economies, and localities.

Whatever the future pace of formal economic cooperation among the economies of the Persian Gulf states, informal economic cooperation already exists, to such an extent that the regional economies within the Gulf are interdependent. The role of a formal cooperative arrangement would be to even out interregional disparities in income and growth.

A central problem for the Gulf states is that of securing the benefits of economies of scale, without weakening the economies of the nations involved. There is a wide variation in the economic structures of the countries under study, and this diversity may increase as economic cooperation advances. For countries such as the UAE and Kuwait, policy intervention will be required to prevent the effects of the transition from a predominantly monoproduct economy—oil—to a more industrial economy from being too destabilizing and inequitable. A reasonably high priority needs to be accorded to regional competitiveness issues in order to avoid or reduce the inefficient or inequitable economic activities that may ensue from competition.

Policy intervention should be framed in the context of long-term strategy. This is underlined by the persistence of regional problems over recent decades in most of the region's economies. The proposed cooperation to enhance the region's competitiveness is likely to bring further pressure, in conjunction with fundamental developmental shifts in the economies of the various states. The issues central to the region discussed here are, accordingly, likely to remain highly relevant to the Persian Gulf economies in the coming years.

REFERENCES

Ahmed, S. A., and H. Donnan (Eds.) (1994). *Islam, Globalization and Post Modernity*. New York: Routledge.

Journal of Commerce (1994). 400: 28255, June 27.

Koon, L. (1971). "Export and Propensity to Save in LDCS." *The Economic Journal*, June.

Maizels, A. (1968). *Export and Economic Growth of Developing Countries*. Cambridge: Cambridge University Press.

"New Services, Same Old Rate Problems" (1993). *Middle East Economic Digest [hereafter MEED]*, March 26.

Porter, M. (Ed.) (1986). *Competition in Global Industries*. Boston: Harvard Business School Press.

"Privatization and Growth of Financial Markets in the Gulf" (1995). *International Financial Law Review*, February.

Temple, M. (1994). *Regional Economics*. New York: St. Martin's Press.

Tyler, W. (1981). "Growth and Export Expansion in Developing Countries: Some Empirical Evidence." *Journal of Development Economics* 9:1.

Weekly, K. J., and R. Aggarwal (1987). *International Business: Operating in the Global Economy*. New York: Dryden Press.

Withiam, G. (1994). *Cornell Hotel and Restaurant Administration Quarterly*, August.

2

The Logic of the Privatization Process: A Selective Study

Monumental economic and political change is sweeping across the Islamic countries of the world. Many of these nations are moving quickly to reorganize their economies according to free market principles. No two countries are exactly alike, and no two can make the transition using exactly the same formula. Nevertheless, there is much to learn by studying the experiences of these countries. Thoughtful analysis and interpretation of the current experiences of these wealth-seeking nations can yield significant benefits.

While privatization efforts are prevailing throughout the Middle East (Mottershaw, 1997), including Bahrain, Kuwait, Oman, Qatar, Saudi Arabia, Turkey, and the UAE, the major theme of this chapter will be privatization as represented by attempts to rid Egypt and Iran of unprofitable and inefficient state-owned enterprises by selling them to domestic or foreign buyers, as well as programs that invite foreign competition in order to break public monopolies or even to provide a heightened measure of competition. The two countries are the largest, most populous nations in the region, with some of the oldest and expansive industrial-base and private-sector experience (Mottershaw, 1997).

INTRODUCTION

Since the early 1980s, privatization has been one of the few economic measures to command broad acceptance internationally from
governments, businesses, and academics. Privatization does not recognize geographic or economic boundaries. It is being implemented
in both poor, developing countries and in wealthy, European countries. The World Bank estimates that privatization is either under way
or being planned in at least fifty countries. Governments sold about
$25 billion worth of assets to private investors in 1990 alone. It is
estimated that a further $30 billion was generated by the sale of state-
owned enterprises in 1991. For example, the magnitude of privatization by the end of the century in the telecommunications industry
is estimated at $145–150 billion (Molano, 1997). Although the oil,
telecommunication, transportation, and chemical sectors are among
the major targets of recent privatization initiatives, the Middle East
has been a latecomer to the privatization arena. Globally it accounts
for less than 1 percent of total divested public enterprises and less
than 3 percent of that in developing countries. Egypt and Iran are
the only countries in the Middle East that have developed a clear and
coherent vision and plan for privatization.

The impact of Egypt and Iran's economic reform programs and
their relevance to the countries' international competitiveness is of
great academic and practical interest. This study makes an original
and timely contribution to understanding the economic progress and
structure of these countries. This study will highlight the process of
privatization. The study further evaluates the international strengths
and weaknesses of the countries in global competition. Thus this
study will assist policy makers to assess the impact of economic recovery programs, privatization, and competitiveness in the region. It
will highlight lessons from Egypt and Iran's programs that may have
great applicability to economic growth and development in other developing countries.

The main objective of the study is to determine whether the economic adjustment program is enabling Egypt and Iran to become
more productive and competitive. Specifically, the study will address
the direct impact of privatization on trade, and the effect of massive
depreciations of currency on prices. In addition, the study will examine whether Iran's economic recovery will be self-sustaining with-

out massive infusion of foreign capital, in the form of concessional loans from donor agencies.

PROGRAM OBJECTIVE

For purpose of this study, policies or programs that lead to a liberalization of trade include those that lessen regulation and emphasize competition, free trade, and protection of intellectual property. Privatization is represented by programs that attempt to rid the state of unprofitable and inefficient state-owned enterprises by selling them to domestic or foreign buyers, as well as programs that invite foreign competition in order to break public monopolies or to provide a heightened measure of competition.

Privatization

Various modalities are being used for this purpose. However, the privatization programs in Egypt and Iran are proceeding at a slower rate than desired. The main reasons are:

- Limited private-sector capacity to absorb a large number of public enterprises.
- Lack of financing, especially long-term credit ("Gas Rich," 1996).
- Lack of clearly stated objectives, and inadequate overall institutional framework for privatization.
- Insecurity about future ownership.
- Limited managerial pool in the private sector.
- Lack of separation between ownership and management.
- Limited capacity of stock exchanges ("Year of the Bull," 1993).
- Restrictive labor laws and excess labor in private sector (Posusney, 1992).
- Lack of interest from foreign investors.
- The usual valuation problems associated with privatization efforts.

The governments are conscious of these problems and are moving to improve the situation. However, further measures to remove uncertainties and develop private sectors should be adopted, and direct sales should be expected. Privatization should be expedited. Privatization in Iran, as elsewhere, is a huge task and will take a number of years to implement.

Measures Suggested to Accelerate and Strengthen Privatization

1. Enhance public understanding and support for privatization by issuing comprehensive policy statements covering program objectives, scope, strategy, industrial and institutional responsibilities, and social safeguards.
2. Use all available modalities (direct sale, auction, management contracts, lease, etc.) rather than just offering shares through stock exchanges, whose capacities are still very limited.
3. Establish a small technical secretariat to support the privatization process.
4. Establish a small treasury account to facilitate the handling of privatization cash flows.
5. Focus privatization efforts on likely successes.
6. Improve implementation of the program by taking steps in the areas of auditing, valuation, and operational efficiency.
7. Improve market information, transparency, and clear regulations.

POLICIES TO SUPPORT PRIVATIZATION AND TRADE LIBERALIZATION

Complementary policies to support privatization should be adopted in two areas. First, policies designed to minimize political resistance to privatization should be adopted. They should prevent high transitional unemployment and economic hardship for the poor, the latter through a well-targeted, cost-effective social safety net. Second, markets have to be deregulated to facilitate relocation of factors of production. The labor codes should be amended and investment restrictions relaxed to eliminate restrictions on firms' capacity to adjust their labor force or expand capacity to make new investments (Merriam and Fluellen, 1992).

The objective of privatization and trade liberalization in Egypt and Iran is to ensure the efficiency of resource allocation across sectors, across firms, and within firms. Such reform is also meant to encourage new investment in activities where the countries have greater comparative advantages and thereby improve the efficiency of investment (Liberman, 1993).

For resource allocation and restructuring to occur, firms must be both willing and able to adjust to changes. Firms' willingness to adjust to changes is based on their expectations about the sustainability of restructuring, and their ability to adjust depends on existing constraints or resource mobility (Erickson and Kavoossi, 1999).

The reason why a firm's willingness to adjust to restructuring is a major issue is that its adjustment decision cannot be reversed without substantial cost. A firm invests time and capital to build a new factory but will not be able to recover even the value of investment if it has to close down or convert it into something else, should the policy be reversed. Policies that enhance sustainability of restructuring also increase a firm's willingness to respond to change. If policies to assist the private sector need time to implement or if their effects take time to work themselves out, the restructuring measures may have to be put in place gradually. In that situation a gradual deregulation may generate more net benefits than a rapid change. However, if the change becomes too gradual, it may lose credibility.

POLICIES TO PROTECT THE NEEDY

The effect of privatization during transition can adversely affect the needy in two ways. Price liberalization and removal of subsidies will likely jeopardize the purchasing power of the poor, which is at a subsistence level. Unemployment is also generated, as firms streamline to stay competitive. There appears to be no organized labor opposition to privatization efforts. This can be partially explained by the weak nature and suppressed conditions of labor unions in the countries.

These effects are likely to hurt the urban lower-middle class and could generate strong political opposition to deregulation and privatization. In order to minimize political resistance to change and thus enhance the credibility of restructuring, it is essential to develop a well-targeted social safety net and facilitate the rapid reabsorption of the transitionally unemployed. However, since developing and implementing a well-targeted social safety net will take considerable time, some slower pace of restructuring is required ("Reform Effort," 1998).

Since the implementation of a well-targeted safety net will take considerable time and price increases from the removal of subsidies and coupons are unacceptably high, it is necessary to delink such a safety net from restructuring. This may be done by increased productivity and by increasing the minimum wage and gradually decreasing subsidized products, or combination of both.

Further, the government can withdraw from direct intervention in the domestic procurement of key commodities. This withdrawal would require a comprehensive overhaul of the procurement and distribution system, currently dominated by official organizations specializing in specific commodities, including oil and gas.

THE OBJECTIVES OF THE PRIVATIZATION

- To break down barriers between the public and private sectors.
- To improve the quality of corporate management.
- To widen the capital base of the countries' industries by allowing greater access to capital markets, less dominated by service-sector borrowing (Seznec, 1995).

The sale of majority public stakes differs from the practice of dispersing only minority holdings. Equally significant is the need for newly privatized firms to raise future financing in domestic or global capital markets rather than through state recapitalization. This will require greater financial restraints, responsibility, transparency, and accountability. It will effectively create financial limits, given the companies' present high levels of indebtedness. Privatization receipts must be used in the first instance to reduce this debt.

The state will remain heavily involved in industrial and service sectors in these countries, especially in these areas:

- Those of strategic interest.
- Those that involve the position of major foundations, in the case of Iran.
- Those where effective competition is not yet perceived as possible.

The governments have set out a series of core activities that will be reserved exclusively or on a preferential basis to the public domain. They include:

- Telecommunication (post, telephone, and telegraph, PTT), even though Iran, with the largest telecommunications market in the Middle East, and

Egypt both have moved to privatize parts of their telecommunication industry, including public switching systems ("Letting Go Speeds," 1998).

- Public-sector broadcasting.
- National airlines, airports, and rail services.
- Oil and gas rights in the mainland, natural gas storage rights. Egypt's oil and gas industry and parts of Iran's are now open to the private sector. Iran is expecting $100 billion of foreign investment in oil, gas, and petrochemicals by the year 2010. Egypt recently opened its oil sector to private investors for the first time, offering them a 35 percent share in the capital of a newly established crude refining and processing firm ("Egypt Lets Privatization," 1998).
- Insurance companies.
- Overall regulation of electricity generation.

This raises the question of continued state conglomerates, which could gradually reexpand their activities under political pressure from future governments less concerned with financial rectitude. The solution of the governments of Presidents Mohammed Khatami and Hosni Mubarak to this could be:

- To place the financial holding companies under treasury control.
- To consider the resulting conglomerate a closed fund limited by law to the initial range of activities identified.

Whether this "anti-politics" strategy will work when post-privatization rationalization and logic begin to bite remains uncertain. Privatization in both countries has been treated as a work in progress. In many areas it is unclear what the precise mechanism will be for bringing companies to the market. The Iranian majlis (parliament) is divided on the issue. The next majlis election may further clarify the national agenda as it relates to privatization. Even in the short term there is considerable political disagreement and jockeying.

The majlis has the responsibility of passing laws and approving the privatization of public property. Some of the key areas to be decided on include:

- Which body will handle the privatization sales and personnel.
- The extent to which the state should remain in the agriculture sector (an issue on which depends the future of farm reform and import subsidies).

- The choice of a strategy to give medium-term stability to the newly privatized firms.

The majlis recently approved legislation confirming the right of foreign companies to own stocks and post registered representatives in the country. In this latter area, governments still have to resolve:

- How far core groups of shareholders will be committed to their holdings for extended periods of time.
- In what areas the governments will retain "lion's share" holdings to influence corporate strategy, given strong political disagreement.

Nevertheless, the reaction of financial markets, both internally and externally, particularly in the case of Egypt, has been positive. Several privatization targets already have minority private-equity stakes, and the share prices of several of these have risen considerably in recent years.

Some solutions to these problems can lead to undesirable consequences. For example, lengthy exclusivity rights will increase a firm's value but may encourage inefficiency. Hence, the role of the governments in providing stability and continuity as well as ongoing support is crucial in the process.

CONCLUSIONS AND RECOMMENDATIONS

As Egypt and Iran adopt more open-market policies, they will need larger volumes of financial assistance. For Egypt and Iran's privatization-related work to evolve along the lines suggested in this chapter and improve international competitiveness, they should adopt the following approach:

1. In transition from the public to private sector, in particular, Iran needs to attract assistance in the form of nongovernmental guaranteed loans and equity investment.
2. Given the risk attendant with privatization and the unleashing of competition, they should be cautious and rigorous in credit and loan accumulation.
3. Given the close link between privatization and capital markets, they need to, where possible, coordinate their privatization and capital market development.

4. They need to enhance the privatization skills of their respective governmental agencies responsible for the process.
5. They need to adopt a flexible approach in selecting privatization projects for foreign assistance ("Egypt Opens," 1998).
6. The private sectors in the countries need to become more actively involved.
7. Iran needs to create an international business council and foster international awareness of itself as a business center.

Many business people believe that privatization is the key to solving the problem of state-owned enterprises in these countries. According to this conventional wisdom, privatization invariably improves corporate management and performance and leads to greater international competitiveness. Experience in a dozen Eastern European companies suggests that this picture is incomplete.

Most newly privatized companies need experienced shareholders to compensate for the weaknesses of managers who have never been exposed to best business practices. Without the support of such shareholders, companies tend to operate very much along the lines of state-owned operations. Managers simply lack the skills and experience to convert a company from its state-run situation to a genuine market orientation. But when these same enterprises receive support from strong, capable shareholders, they have shown that they can perform to international standards and even outperform some Western companies ("Overcoming Geography," 1998).

Iran needs to put its program completely in place, if for no other reason than to create and attract the kind of strong investors who can provide leadership, experience, and direction. The positive effects of privatization are far from automatic.

As privatization efforts unfold in these countries, several key research questions gain greater urgency:

- How does the microeconomic performance of state-owned companies, such as efficiency, impact the likelihood that a privatization program will be approved?
- How do macroeconomic conditions in Egypt and Iran, such as external debt and inflation, shape their privatization policies and their successful implementation?
- How does the political environment effect the implementation of privatization policies differently in different countries?

REFERENCES

"Egypt Lets Privatization into Oil Sector" (1998). *Privatization News*, June 15–21.

"Egypt Opens Insurance Sector to Foreign Investment" (1998). *Middle East Business Intelligence*, January 5.

Erickson, C. J., and M. Kavoossi (1999). "Global Telecommunications Competition and Strategy Choice for Emerging Markets." In D. Despotis and C. Zoponidis (Eds.), *Integrating Technology and Human Decisions: Global Bridges into the 21st Century*. Athens, Greece: New Technologies Publications.

"Gas Rich and Credit Hungry" (1996). *Euromoney*, May.

Kikeri, Sunita, et al. (1992). *Privatization: The Lessons of Experience*, Washington, D.C.: World Bank.

"Letting Go Speeds Up Expansion: Telecommunications Privatization" (1998). *MEED*, March 13.

Liberman, I. W. (1993). "Privatization: The Theme of the 1990s." *Columbia Journal of World Business* 28: 1, 7–17.

McDonald, Kevin (1993). "Why Privatization Is Not Enough." *Harvard Business Review*, June.

Merriam, J. G., and A. J. Fluellen (1992). "Arab World Privatization: Key to Development." *Arab Studies Quarterly* 14:2 and 3 (Spring/Summer).

Mirsepassi, Nasser (1989). *Managing Human Resources and Labor Relations* (7th ed.). Tehran, Iran: Globe Publishing.

Molano, Walter (1997). *The Logic of Privatization: The Case of Telecommunications in the Southern Cone of Latin America*. Westport, Conn.: Greenwood Press, p. 4.

Mottershaw, Elizabeth (1997). "Gulf Funds Primed for Privatization." *MEED*, June 13.

——— (1997). "Gulf Infrastructure Gets a Shake-Up." *MEED*, June 13.

"Overcoming Geography and Statism" (1998). *Institutional Investor*, July.

Posusney, Marsha (1992). "Labor as an Obstacle to Privatization," In I. Harik and O. Sullivan (Eds.), *Privatization and Liberalization in the Middle East*. Indiana University Press.

"Privatization: Experience and Pitfalls" (1993). *Tadbir*, June.

"Reform Effort Needs to Shift Up a Gear" (1998). *MEED*, June 5.

Seznec, Jean-Françoise (1995). *Columbia Journal of World Business*, Fall.

"Year of the Bull: Tehran's Stock Exchange" (1993). *Banker*, February.

3

Determinants of Consumer Behavior in an Islamic Society

This chapter discusses the determinants of consumer behavior in an Islamic society. It also analyzes the dimensions of the religious and cultural context of consumer behavior. It concludes, more specifically, with a study of the integration of Islamic society and specific consumer behavior. The purposes of this chapter are to analyze the religious and cultural framework that provides the context for marketing practices; to examine the causal relationship between this context and consumer behavior; and to review the consumer market opportunities and constraints in Islamic countries.

Despite many political uncertainties, the Middle Eastern countries' rapid economic growth is generating an increasing consumer demand for modern products. The Islamic countries' markets are neither monolithic nor mysterious, nor too costly to penetrate, as many Western companies believe.

The image of primitive Muslim bazaars has changed into one of more sophisticated centers of trade. Modern consumer products, such as automobiles, home video systems, personal computers, and other electronic appliances, including satellite dishes and digital television, are increasingly popular items.

Modernization encompasses the application of technology to the process of material and nonmaterial development, through innovative and appropriate products that respond to consumer needs and desires.

Yet the rise of modernization does not necessarily correspond to a decline of traditional values. Many Asian countries, including Japan and Singapore, are examples of a mixture of modernity and tradition. That is also true of most of the Persian Gulf states. While traditional in their nonmaterial, significating components of their cultures, they have emerged fully capable of utilizing state-of-the-art consumer and industrial products.

The move to modernization is not limited to any one country. Market prospects in Kuwait and Saudi Arabia are expanding rapidly. While these countries remain fairly restricted and closed to the outside world, they are some of the fastest-growing markets in the area. Rapid market growth in the region has encouraged foreign marketers and created outstanding business opportunities, which are becoming increasingly competitive. This competitive business environment, as discussed in chapter 1, has promoted a willingness to market consumer-oriented products through more innovative and creative entry strategies.

THE ISLAMIC BUSINESS ENVIRONMENT

The management of Muslim markets also requires understanding of variations in governmental attitudes toward access to domestic markets. Many Muslim nations have adopted an open-door policy for foreign investors and exporters. This spirit of open access has spread throughout the Middle East, with the exceptions of Libya, Syria, and Algeria. However, private ownership grows in strength in Iran, Iraq, Egypt, Saudi Arabia, Kuwait, Jordan, Morocco, Tunisia, Turkey, and other, smaller Persian Gulf states, including the United Arab Emirates.

Many entrepreneurs in the private sectors of these countries are responding to market demands for modern products. Both foreign and domestic businesses must begin to recognize the need to apply appropriate marketing strategies and to position themselves to capture new market segments through a better understanding of the determinants of consumer behavior in Islamic society. Dimensions of religious and cultural context of consumer behavior must be specifically analyzed to determine the degree of integration of specifically consumer behavior and the dominant Islamic paradigm.

Little has been written in the West, in either the academic or popular press, about the subject. The vast majority of the empirical and conceptual literature has focused on such issues as the Islamic economy. The extent to which marketing practices account for success or failure of Islamic economies has been generally neglected in the literature.

ISLAMIC SOCIETY

Islamic rationalism is founded on the ideological belief in the oneness of God and in the unity of Islam with *all* other aspects of life. In this belief, human life is conceived as a whole, oriented toward one ultimate goal. This goal has many expressions in Islamic faith and literature, such as serving God, worshiping God, etc. In fact, all of these expressions may be said to be efforts toward obtaining the consent of God.

Islamic rationalism has succeeded in handling many problems of human behavior that Western economic rationalism has failed to explain. Because of its historical background, Western capitalist rationalism is alien to the Islamic economic scheme and behavioral attitudes. Despite this lack of close contact with the Western materialistic economic system, Islamic rationalism has not ignored the importance of man's material wants, needs, and satisfactions.

Islam is not satisfied with merely awakening human consciousness and putting it on the right track; rather, it creates the environmental conditions necessary for the proper functioning of this consciousness. Therefore, the study of consumer behavior in an Islamic society must include an analysis of the socio-economic context and atmosphere provided by Islamic teachings—that is, of the determinants of Islamic consciousness. "In the scheme of Islamic ethics, a free man establishes three simultaneous relationships; with God, with his own self, and with the society. . . . [T]the basic axiom of unity, equilibrium, free will and responsibility summarizes all the basic aspects of these relationships" (Naqvi, 1994).

CONTEXTUAL FRAMEWORK OF CONSUMER BEHAVIOR AND PROMOTION IN AN ISLAMIC SOCIETY

In order to understand the context of consumer behavior in an Islamic society, certain assumptions must be made (Kahf, 1981). An Islamic society is defined as a society where the Islamic laws and institutions prevail and where the majority of individuals believe in the Islamic ideology and practice its way of life as embodied in a code of conduct and ethics. Such a society would be quite different from many contemporary Islamic societies. A number of Islamic societies, in practice, appear to have become something less than Islamic, in the fashion in which many Western, secular societies have evolved— societies where a color TV adds more to one's life than do the strict directives of the Prophet Mohammed or the Koran.

Throughout history, societies have imposed certain limitations and constraints on the goods and services made available to the consumer. The use of certain commodities is sometimes forbidden by legislation, prohibited by religion, or simply impossible because of the level of economic and industrial development. Alcohol prohibition (in the 1920s) in the United States, the banning of smoking among the members of the Mormon church (Church of Jesus Christ of Latter-Day Saints), and restrictions on beef consumption among Hindus are a few examples.

Consumer behavior in an Islamic society is dominated by four general principles: the belief in the last day (*Akhira*); the Islamic concept of success; the Islamic concept of wealth (Kavoossi, 1988); and the moral dimensions of consumer behavior, such as limitations placed on consumption, or principles of caring for others (Kahf, 1981).

Islam extends the time horizon of Muslims beyond death. Belief in the day of judgment (*Akhira*) extends the time horizon of one's decisions. Life before death and after death are closely interrelated, in a sequential manner. This has two effects, as far as consumer behavior is concerned. First, the outcome of a choice of action is composed of two parts: its immediate effect in this life, and its later effect in the life to come (Kavoossi, 1988). Second, the number of alternative uses of one's income is increased by all the benefits that would be gained only in the hereafter. In other words, opportunity cost is extended and gains further dimensions. Examples of such alternative uses are interest-free lending, giving charity to the poor and the needy, spending for the welfare of the future generations, improvement of one's life even when this has no immediate benefit for the individual, promotion and perpetuation of goodness, etc. (Chapra, 1986). It must be noted that charitable contributions or other benevolent acts are expenses not necessarily counted toward tax deductions or other material benefits. Thus, many alternative uses of one's income may have positive utility in the Islamic society, whereas their utility in the capitalist system may be zero or negative.

Success is defined in Islam in terms of servitude, serving the wishes of God, and not in terms of the accumulation of wealth. The concept of successful life in Islam does not entail acquisition of more and more material goods. The real success of a person lies not in building up an inventory of articles; virtue, righteousness, and service to God are the keys to success. Virtue and righteousness can be achieved through good actions and purification of thought and behavior. No doubt, the Koran speaks of the material resources of this world being consumed and enjoyed by mankind, but they are basically a means to life in this world. They are not an end in themselves. Service and obedience to God may be rendered by the positive use of human capabilities and resources given by God.

Maximization of satisfaction with minimum resources is highly encouraged. According to Islamic teachings, if a man really wants to serve God, the utilization of the natural and human resources made available to him is not only a privilege but also a duty and obligation presented by God (Vassilliou, 1983). Therefore, material progress and perfection are in themselves moral values in Islam (Shilling, 1983). However, the source of pride in early Islamic society was self-imposed deprivation for the welfare of others. The Prophet Mohammed taught contentment (*Gana*) and the subduing of demands for material resources. The attitude of *Shukr* (thanksgiving) implies that resources should not be wasted prematurely. Instead, for example, they should be utilized until their utility is outlived. One should not keep an inventory of clothes and should not discard a garment prematurely. Maximization of success may be reduced to the attainment of two objectives: the satisfaction derived from the consumption of goods and services, and the enrichment of life in the hereafter by spending for the sake of God. The Koran has condemned people who spend their life in pursuit of pleasure (material and sensuous) (11: 116). It discourages extravagance.

The concept of wealth and income is unique in Islam. Belongings, whether perceived as wealth or income, are a bounty from God, and not evil. Heaven is not just for the poor; rich men may also find the doors wide open. Wealth is a tool that may be used for good or evil (Khan, 1985). Poverty in some instances is associated with disbelief, whereas riches are considered a gift from God (ibid.). Since riches are from Him, they must be used for the benefit and satisfaction of human wants. This is an implication of service to God. Given this relationship between wealth and income, consumption is defined as a tool to buy goods and services, which bring about satisfaction; they should be used for that purpose and not hoarded. Real income is defined as the total of that which is used for the purchase of goods and services that produce immediate satisfaction in this life, plus that which is given away for causes that in turn enrich one's life in the hereafter (Rajaee, 1983).

Consumer behavior in an Islamic society can be described as the maximization of success, and demand control. Success may be narrowly defined as corresponding with consumer choice and service to God. The maximization of success by the consumer is subject to income constraint determined by the level of disposable income.

Islam considers lawfully acquired wealth and income to be subject to the protection of the law; however, one may forfeit this protection if he misuses the wealth or income. Extravagance, waste, and general abuse of money lead the community to attribute a poor character to him, since he, with his immorality, is damaging the interest of the community. Such a person may forfeit his wealth to his community, which may limit his use of it to that part required to meet his basic needs. This may provide the theoretical grounds for government intervention in private wealth management.

The Koran has condemned both extravagance (*Israf*) and miserliness (*Bukhl*), and it has encouraged the adoption of an attitude of moderation in consumption. *Israf* leads to waste of resources, and *Bukhl* locks away the resources from the production process, leading to deprivation. Obsolescence of articles because of changing fashion or technology leads to extravagance, in most cases. In the Islamic market, such obsolescence would be reduced to a minimum, possibly diminishing innovation. "New and improved" will take on a new meaning.

Shariah, Islamic law, provides a network of ethical and moral rules of behavior, including the behavior of all participants in the market. It requires that these norms and rules be internalized and adhered to by all participants before their entrance into the market. Not all demands are recognized as legitimate causes for production. Also, demand in itself does not determine price; price ought to be determined by observance of all Islamic codes of ethics. Prices must be kept at a reasonable level to make basic goods and services available to the public. The public sector can intervene when there are distortions.

Shariah introduces a moral dimension into consumer behavior by defining *Halal* (lawful), *Haram* (unlawful), and *Makrough* (conditional) articles. A number of activities cannot be permitted, on ethical grounds. For example, one cannot spend on alcohol, pork, gambling, silk, gold, or silver (there are exceptions for women). Consumer sovereignty is thus compromised in the Islamic society. In fact, the theory of consumer sovereignty conflicts with the Islamic concept of *Towhid* (the unity of God), which suggests that the resources of the earth are the creation of God and that He alone has the right to decide its mode of utilization. A consumer in an Islamic society would allocate his income on *Halal* articles, with none to *Haram* articles.

CONSUMER BEHAVIOR AND INCOME ALLOCATION FOR CONSUMER GOODS

The consumption function is usually defined in capitalist economic literature as the relationship between income and the consumption of goods and services. These goods and services constitute only one part of spending, namely, spending on goods and services that bring about immediate satisfaction. In an Islamic society, the second component of spending, spending for the sake of God, is not accounted for in the consumption function. The term "spending" refers to these two components together. Spending is distinguished from investment in that the latter affects the level of wealth, whereas the former affects real income. One is not to borrow money to purchase nonessential material goods. For example, a CD player or a VCR may not fit the definition of essentials. An automobile, however, as a basic mode of transportation, may qualify.

A life of luxury and material acquisition is held in low esteem in an Islamic society. Consequently, demand for luxury items should remain at low levels. The general public demands the basic necessities of life; therefore, resources should be allocated, primarily, for the production of necessities. It is desirable to produce the basic necessities of life at low cost and in large quantity, so that most of the population may be able to avail themselves of them. Luxuries and comforts would be in low demand not only because of the value systems but because the government may levy heavy taxes to discourage their production, promotion, or importation into the society.

An Islamic society holds goods of high quality and durability in high esteem. The entrepreneur should produce articles of high durability, so that replacement is not needed after a short time. Moreover, an entrepreneur's efforts to create demand by creating a desire to change, or by inspiring a change of fashion, would violate the ethical norms of the society. As a result, it would become a norm that no articles should be abandoned until fully worn out.

In a modern-day context, the Islamic market would keep the demand for consumables down by encouraging the production of high-durability goods and by discouraging obsolescence due to change in taste and fashion. In early Muslim economies, durability of products was considerably greater than at present. Household products were produced in such a manner that they remained in use for generations (Khan, 1985). Whether there is a manufacturing component of an Islamic society remains to be further investigated, to develop a possible Islamic manufacturing theory.

In the present situation, an Islamic market would reintroduce both these factors, high-durability and obsolescence, into the production process. Products of greater durability would be produced, and changes in fashion would be condemned as social vice.

The question arises: how would the economy be maintained, if the process of creation of demand is suppressed? No simple answer can be given. However, it seems that the mainstay of an Islamic society in the past has been *Jihad* ("holy struggle"), an ongoing struggle for progress; the economy was maintained by developing resources for *Jihad*. The Koran strongly argues in favor of a creation of a strong military force for the defense of Islam (ibid.). In a modern Islamic economy, preparation for *Jihad* would expend resources not only on the army and armaments but also on research and development.

DETERMINANTS OF SPENDING DECISIONS

A discussion of consumer spending decisions requires an understanding of those institutions considered integral to the socioeconomic structure of an Islamic society.

Khoms and *Zakat* are institutions that are assumed to be a part of the socioeconomic structure. *Zakat* means purification or growth. The concept of *Zakat* is derived from the Islamic belief that all things belong to God. Human possessions are purified through the act of *Zakat*, in which one allocates a portion of one's wealth for those who are in need. *Khoms* is an annual payment equal to one-fifth of a Muslim's capital.

Khoms and *Zakat* are collected and distributed in accordance with Islamic injunctions requiring a *Khoms* and *Zakat* fund as a department of the executive branch of government. *Zakat* is considered as a constant ratio of net worth, while *Khoms* is one-fifth of income, and there are no restrictions on the collection and distribution of these two. The ownership of *Khoms* and *Zakat* must be transferred to the public; it should not remain in the hands of the authorities. However, *Zakat* can be collected or dispensed in the form of consumer goods or producers' goods.

Riba, or interest, because it is prohibited by law, influences consumer spending patterns in a given Islamic society. Every predetermined fixed or variable rate of return is viewed as interest and therefore *Riba*; thus the rate of interest on loans should always be zero. There is no distinction as far as the prohibition of interest is concerned between producer credit and consumer credit.

An Islamic economy changes the pattern of income distribution through *Zakat* and prohibition of *Riba*, worker participation in profits, and the law of inheritance, property rights, and ownership. Greater purchasing power is therefore instilled among the poorer sections of society. Production concentrates on the basic necessities of life, which have relatively inelastic demand, as compared to the demand for creature comforts and luxuries.

In order to understand better the determinants of spending decisions, one must study the effects of *Zakat* and *Riba* on income allocation between saving and spending. *Zakat* influences both payer and recipient. Since *Zakat* is imposed on accumulated net worth and not only on income, the wealth owner must increase his savings in order to prevent the level of his wealth from decreasing. *Zakat* is far more than an obligation imposed by God on the faithful for the general welfare of the *Umma* (Islamic community), or a tax promoted by the state for the sake of collecting revenues for its own purpose (Cummings et al., 1980). *Zakat* penalizes idle wealth. This effect tightens the relationship between saving decisions and investment and brings these two decisions closer to each other as far as the time span between them is concerned.

PROMOTION

The promotion function in an Islamic economy has been recognized on the basis that all consumer information be supplied separately from all other articles, services, and information. The consumer might pay for the cost of such information, but he would be aware of this cost. The cost of information, thus, would not be concealed in the cost of product or in the cost of other information. Accordingly, the information media would not carry any advertisements (Khan, 1985).

Advertising information would be available on a professional basis, so that it would contain hard facts about products or services. Islam prohibits sellers from promoting sales by false claims. Thus, in an Islamic society the seller would make the buyer aware of the negative aspects of his products. Advertising, in an Islamic society, would be an announcement of the availability, price, quality, and other attributes of a product or service.

The producers of the same item or a close substitute would be given a similar opportunity, in a standardized form, to advertise their products or services, to prevent an appearance of monopoly in the supply of information for some economically powerful product. A reform of the above would probably involve the introduction of new methods of the media and creative financing.

CONCLUSION

In contrast to non-Islamic capitalist economics, Islamic theory considers the consumer to be a seeker of the good life in this world and the world hereafter. It must be noted that the accumulation and maintenance of wealth is not entirely undesirable or negative.

The Islamic system, by virtue of its very nature, maintains a high rate of savings. The inherent forces of the Islamic system make the investment perspective an integral part of the savings decision. Saving is positively related to investment opportunities and expectations. This relationship implies that at times of declining investment expectations, saving will decline, and consumption will rise. This in turn increases demand.

Khoms and *Zakat* serve as taxes on income and accumulated wealth. This kind of tax plays an important role in the functioning of the Islamic system, even as an incentive for investment. However, at the same time that it encourages the consumer–wealth owner to maintain the level of his wealth by increasing his savings, the distribution of *Zakat* increases the disposable income of the recipient, thus raising his consumption. This system puts the hand of the economic policy on a large portion of the society's output. *Zakat* has to be collected and distributed every year, giving the economic authority a role in influencing the trends of economic activity, as well as its level.

While Islamic societies have adapted to modern marketing practices, they have yet to achieve an organic balance between consumerism and the Islamic values that bind these societies together (Mehmet, 1990). The existence of a weak civil society in many Islamic nations has further hindered this process.

It can be reasonably argued that in most Western industrial free-market economies, particularly that of the United States, the dominant societal organizing principle is the foundation of the economics. In Middle Eastern Islamic societies, however, there exists a serious challenge and tension caused by economic forces attempting to dominate the cultural and religious components of these societies. In short, the societal process is in flux and inherently less stable than in the West. However, it is less unstable than those of many of the newly emerging markets of Eastern Europe.

While consumer determinism is on the ascendant, the outcome of its confrontation with Islamic values and emphasis on spiritual and nonmaterial aspects of life remains to be seen. It is not quite clear which is going to be the winner. However, no matter which wins, the winner and loser (consumerism or Islam) will be changed and possibly radicalized and revitalized.

REFERENCES

A Business Guide to the Kingdom of Saudi Arabia (1996). Washington, D.C.: Royal Embassy of Saudi Arabia Commercial Office.

Chapra, M. U. (1986). *Towards a Just Monetary System*. Leicester, U.K.: Islamic Foundation.

Cummings, J. T., H. Askari, and A. Mustafa (1980). "Islam and Modern Economic Change." In John Esposito (Ed.), *Islam and Development*. Syracuse, NY: Syracuse University Press, pp. 25–49.

The Information Revolution and the Arab World: Its Impact on State and Society (1998). Abu Dhabi, UAE: The Emirates Center for Strategic Studies and Research.

Kahf, M. (1981). "A Contribution to the Theory of Consumer Behavior in Islamic Society." In K. Ahmad (Ed.), *Studies in Islamic Economics*. Jeddah, Saudi Arabia: International Center for Research on Islamic Economics.

Kahn, A. (1985). "Resource Allocation in an Islamic Economy." *Islamic Quarterly* (Fourth Quarter).

Kavoossi, M. (1988). "Islamic Interest Free Banking and Populist Islamic Ideology: Times of Transition." In R. Aggarawal and C. Crespy (Eds.), *Midwest Review of International Business Research*. Chicago: Academy of International Business.

LeClair, M. (1997). *Regional Integration and Global Free Trade*. London: Avebury.

Mehmet, O. (1990). *Islamic Identity and Development*. New York: Routledge.

Naqvi, Sayed Haider (1994). *Islam, Economics and Society*. London: Kegan Paul International.

Noreng, O. (1997). *Oil and Islam: Social and Economic Issues*. New York: John Wiley and Sons.

Rajaee, F. (1983). *Islamic Values and World View*. Lanham, Md.: University Press of America.

Sanaie, A. (1996). "Marketing in Islamic Countries: Iran's Case Study." *Journal of International Marketing and Marketing Research* 21:3.

Shilling, N. A. (1983). *Marketing in the Arab World*. Dallas, Tex.: Inter-Crescent.

Vassilliou, G. (1983). *Marketing in the Middle East*. London: McCorquodele.

4

An Empirical Investigation of the Role of Languages in Advertisements in the Middle East: The Emerging Challenges and Problems

M. Kavoossi and J. Frank

To market successfully a product or service internationally, one must have a firm grasp of the ways cross-cultural differences in communication influence the creation, implementation, and outcomes of advertising campaigns. With much of the global industrial expansion and promotion now focused on the Middle East, from direct marketing of water sports equipment and cosmetics, to liquor, tobacco, food and beverage, and health care products cultural differences will affect not only the internal conduct and organization of multinational firms and consumer attitudes toward product "country of origin," but also affect foreign and domestic marketers' competitive strategies vis-à-vis advertising in all media. It might be expected, therefore, that cultural differences will also affect competitive advertising strategies used in foreign and domestic markets.[1]

An analysis of a sampling of print advertisements gathered from major periodicals distributed in the Persian Gulf region supports that expectation, as we discovered when—for comparative purposes—we examined the messages in the texts for elements of a persuasional style that has been shown to be characteristic of Arab rhetoric, with their emphasis on evaluative or factual content. Focusing on the texts and the visual strategies used, we found that religious and social values and attitudes shape the language and the images that appear in print advertising in the Middle East. Further, our investigation on the Persian Gulf points to less market segmentation, variability, and heterogeneity in this geographic region, so that, all in all, our conclusion is that marketing in this region shows a relationship between the information content of print advertisements and language.

The relationship between language and culture has been a major issue of concern for psychology and anthropology for some time, since Sapir and Crocker (1977) first advanced their hypothesis that language determines, or at least influences, the way we look at our world. Although a range of studies have challenged the validity of both linguistic determinism and linguistic relativism on empirical and theoretical grounds, recent reconceptualizations of the language-culture relationship have focused more on the sociocultural context of language and culture acquisition. Such studies suggest that a more useful approach is to assume there is an interactional relationship between them. According to these views, cognitive processes affect our language use, yet language also shapes our inferences and value judgments, by virtue of its inherent involvement in the process of acquiring cultural practices.

In the case of marketing in the Middle East, such conclusions have important implications for identifying and evaluating the impact of cross-cultural differences in developing campaigns designed to cross national boundaries, although few studies have specifically focused on the specific ways differences in attitudes and perceptions are actually conveyed in advertising communications. Indeed, little attention in general has been paid by market researchers to the relationship between culturally conditioned attitudes and beliefs and language in international contexts, and the important role that variances in these perceptions may play in the success of international advertising strategies. This is true although a review of recent literature indicates a growing interest in the contents of these advertising messages (see, for example, Rice and Lu, 1988; Gilly, 1988), and it is these studies that prompted our own investigation.

Study after study points to market segmentation, variability, and heterogeneity, and suggests that social variables, in combination with cultural values and attitudes, may be predictors of consumer behavior. Yet, since the success of international marketing may depend on worldwide similarities in markets for products or services, regardless of their point of origin, the practice of advertising the same product in the same way in all markets of the world (standardized international advertising) is likely to proliferate. For companies operating in the Persian Gulf region, is market homogeneity a reasonable assumption?

Inspired by the recent research that emphasizes the sociocultural context of language, we examined and categorized the style and approach used in some Persian Gulf advertisements, in order to identify some features of advertising messages that may be relevant to the success of domestic and international firms operating in the Middle East region. Our corpus of forty magazine advertisements was gathered from four regional periodicals. The advertisements were mainly, or exclusively, written in Arabic, with a small number wholly in languages other than Arabic (English, Italian, French). For advertisements in the former category, we primarily relied on translations from the Arabic provided by an independent translator. The frequency of distribution and categories of products and services, in our judgment, fairly represented that which occurs in modern everyday life; they were advertisements that a citizen of Kuwait, Bahrain, or Egypt might commonly see or read.

To analyze the advertisements, we used a combination of methods. First, the message content of the advertisements was analyzed, using the Resnick and Stern classification system, which determines the level of advertising information based on fourteen cues (e.g., Madden et al. 1986); the notional and graphic content of the ads were handled via definitions and categories that we developed, based on the assumption that advertising reflects normative social roles and cultural norms. Finally, the text was analyzed to explore some elements of persuasional style that have been shown to be characteristic of Arabic rhetoric or that reflect emphasis on evaluative versus factual content. The findings of our study are presented below. While the conclusions must necessarily be tentative, given the small number of advertisements in the sample, the findings lend credence to the idea that certain aspects of Middle East and (specifically) Arab culture and language will drive international marketers to "think globally, act locally."

INFORMATIONAL CONTENT

Like other analysts utilizing the Resnik-Stern criteria, we considered an ad to be informative if it contained at least one of the fourteen

Table 4.1 Distribution of Informational Cues			
	Products (N=28) number/% of sample	Services (N=12) number/% of sample	Total (N=40) number/% of sample
Ads containing 0 cues	1/2.5%	1/2.5%	2/5%
Ads containing > 1 cue	27/96%	11/92%	38/95%
Ads containing > 2 cues	17/61%	4/33%	21/53%
Ads containing > 3 cues	9/32%	1/8%	10/25%
Ads containing > 4 cues	4/15%	0	4/15%

information cues. By this measure, as Table 4.1 shows, not all the ads were informative, although the percentage of ads that contained at least one cue was high: 95 percent.

As Table 4.1 demonstrates, when the number of cues was raised to at least two, a little more than 50 percent of the advertisements qualified as informative. The frequency drops substantially after three cues; only one-quarter of the ads qualified by this measure, and only four ads in the corpus contained four or more informational cues. We also analyzed the data to determine if the frequency of cues was linked to the type of offering: products or services. The informational content, if measured by occurrence of informational cues, was greater for products (appliances, clothing) than for services (air travel, banking).

These results differ from recent content analyses of magazine ads in other countries. For example, Madden et al. analyzed U.S. and Japanese magazine advertisements and found that 75 percent of U.S. ads contained at least one informational cue, while only 39 percent contained at least two cues (Madden et al., 1986). In contrast, Rice and Lu analyzed Chinese magazine advertisements, to find that 100 percent of their sample was informative by the criteria of "at least one"; 77.7 percent qualified as informative when the requirement was raised to "at least two"; and 3.8 percent of their sample had "at least five cues" (Stern et al., 1981). We also found that ads for products contained a higher percentage of cues overall than those for services; the difference is appreciable when the criteria was "two or more." We conjecture that historically limited exposure to a large range of products and services, combined with a comparatively greater need for decision making in these areas once exposure begins, would make likely a need for more information, especially if those who are in a

Table 4.2 Frequency of Informational Cues (N=40)		
Cue Type	% Ads with Cue	Percent
1. Availability	13	32.5
2. Performance	16	40.0
3. Quality	15	37.5
4. Price	3	7.5
5. Independent Research	0	0
6. Packaging	9	22.5
7. Guarantee of Warranties	6	15
8. New Ideas	3	7.5
9. Components	5	12.5
10. Safety	0	0
11. Taste	0	0
12. Nutritious	0	0
13. Company Research	0	0
14. Special Offers	0	0
Total Number of Cues = 74; Mean = 1.85		

position to make decisions view advertising primarily as a vehicle for providing information.[2]

Table 4.2 shows the frequency of occurrence of the fourteen informational cues, and percentage of the sample. As can be seen, product or service availability, performance, and quality were the most commonly used cues; they appeared with approximately the same frequency (30 percent) in the ads.

With the exception of packaging, guarantees, and components cues, used in 22.5 percent, 15 percent, and 12.5 percent of the ads, respectively, information on price and new ideas were rarely found. No information on independent research, safety, taste, nutrition, company research, or special offers was offered in any advertisement. The total number of cues found was seventy-four, and the average number of cues per ad was 1.85. Again, these findings vary from previous studies that assessed the information content of American, Japanese, and Chinese ads. Rice and Lu found 2.26 cues per ad in their sampling of Chinese magazines, which they report was considerably higher than the information levels reported in content analyses of American and Japanese magazine advertisements (Gumperz and Cook-Gumperz, 1981).

RELATIONSHIP OF INFORMATION CONTENT TO LANGUAGE USE AND CULTURE

Some aspects of rhetorical meaning, or communicative intent, will be reflected in word choice or word order, some in grammar, and some in punctuation. Differences in syntactic, grammatical, and stylistic features and devices across texts, hence, may represent writers' efforts to exploit cross-cultural differences in sociolinguistic norms in order to convey meaning. Display advertisements also communicate visually and symbolically underlying motivations and cultural preferences, which differ from culture to culture. In general, advertising that focuses on perceived lifestyles or relies on personal evaluations or opinions to "persuade" will tend to vary across cultures, while advertising that appeals to a culturally "marginal" audience or appeals to the highest socioeconomic class will be relatively similar.

Arabic rhetorical style is more "presentational" than "logically" persuasive in style (Johnston, 1983). That is, one's style of presenting an argument or the way words are arranged and used, matters as much or more than logical underpinnings for an argument or a display of factual, reasoned argumentation in the Western, Aristotelian tradition. Thus, a presentational style relies chiefly on the power of words to evoke powerful emotional and cognitive responses in readers. The force of the argument is carried by the intrinsic properties of language itself.

Since words are crucial in this style of persuasion and the writer's goal is to convince readers through sensory and emotional involvement, such features as sound and word repetitions, use of detail, syntactic parallelism, visual/abstract metaphors, and a variety of evaluative devices are most appropriate to the situation and indeed typify Arabic rhetoric. For example, in an advertisement for Seiko watches we find the following text (translated from the Arabic):

> Fill every day of your life with golden moments,
> the moments of Seiko . . .
>> Enjoy the times you deserve.

The word "moments" is repeated, to emphasize and prepare the reader in advance for the metaphor found in the last phrase—the "times" deserved by the reader. By Resnik and Stern's criteria, the information content of this ad is nil; none of the fourteen informational cues are used. The advertiser has apparently presumed readers will be able to infer all that is needed to make a positive (i.e., persuasive) connection between Seiko (brand identification) and watches—because the reader is expected to feel they deserve "golden moments."

Another example is an ad for Parker pens: the banner is written in Arabic script: "The magnificence of the Arabic word shines in its written form." Then follows the copy, in print form:

As a symbol of its great admiration of the "Dhad" language, Parker, one of the prominent international producers of quality pens, expresses its appreciation for the eternal beauty of Arabic writing.
. . . Parker pens for the best-known language the world ever knew.

Below the text is a photograph of a Parker pen, positioned as if held in the hand. The Parker logo is strong, appearing twice in the ad, at the top and at the bottom, in combination with the English word "PARKER" in bold caps.

At the same time, analysis of the data also indicates that readers are relatively sophisticated. In cases where the text, in the author's judgement, was produced solely for the targeted market and only the graphic or illustrative elements were obviously "borrowed" from other sources (such as promotional photographs provided by a foreign manufacturer, or purchased "stock" photographs), the ad was considered "domestic," or nonstandardized. Analysis revealed that 64 percent of the ads were placed by international, as opposed to domestic, companies. This finding lends support to Banks's cross-national analysis of advertising expenditures; he speculates that entrepreneurs in countries in the bloom of economic and social development might be tempted into highly expansive advertising. This might account for the trend toward relatively higher volumes of standardized advertising (72 percent) placed in Egyptian magazines to target a local, regional audience.

Moreover, advertising campaigns that aim at the well-to-do, upper-socioeconomic classes have traditionally been exceptions to the rule that buying motivations related to perceived lifestyles differ across cultures and are therefore difficult to transfer. The products and services that fall into this exceptional class are luxury automobiles, travel, jewelry and watches, perfumes, imported beverages, and cigarettes; these have consistent appeal to the up-market segment of multinational populations and often are advertised with a consistent (i.e., centralized) creative approach. The results of our analysis bear this out; in the advertisements studied, it is the luxury items, such as expensive pens, watches, cars, tobacco, and imported Scotch (included among foods and beverages) that are "standardized."

Another way to assess the relative sophistication of readers is to examine the frequency with which languages other than Arabic appear in the ads. It was found that very few ads were "100 percent" Arabic; a majority contained at least some English, even if that usage was reserved for the brand name or name of the company, or appeared on the product package. Indeed, 70 percent of the ads expected readers to know some English or other foreign language. Also, and not unexpectedly, given the numbers of international companies who advertise in these magazines, almost twice as many advertisers of products, as opposed to services, used English in their advertisements.

Further, when the data was analyzed to compare products/services by origin to "use of language," not surprisingly, 60 percent of the seventeen (out of twenty nine ads) that contained English or some other language were international companies, while only two of the twelve ads in Arabic, or only 5 percent, were international companies. Moreover, of the two ads that were solely in English, and the one in Italian, all represented companies from wholly non-native-English-speaking countries: Aeroflot (the Russian airline) and Austrian Airlines (in English), and Blancpain watches (French watches, ad in Italian with some French). No obvious attempt was made in any of these ads to make the theme, copy, or illustration "culture specific" to the local market. Thus, it can be presumed that a good number of potential consumers have at least some proficiency in English, or a European language, and that they are experienced enough to recognize (and identify with) international company brands (e.g., AT&T, Parker, Swissair).

In some ads, given the frequency of informational cues, their distribution and type in relation to the source of the advertisement, and the language used, two explanations—potentially equally correct—are possible. An analysis of the data suggests that a relatively sophisticated (i.e., well-traveled, experienced) and wealthy class of consumers is being targeted by these advertisements—readers who would expect a lower information content for international goods and a higher in-

Table 4.3 Cues for Products or Services Related to Advertisement Origination			
Product/Service	# Ads	# Int'l Origin	#/% of Int'l "Standardized"
Products			
Tobacco	3	3	3/100%
Jewelry (watches, etc.)	2	2	2/100%
Misc. Small Consumer (pen, razor)	4	4	3/75%
Electric Appliance/Durables	8	7	1/14%
Industrial Products (paper, detergent)	4	1	1/100%
Food (including imported beverages, other)	3	1	1/100%
Clothing	3	0	0
Services			
Travel	8	7	7/100
Banking/Financial	3	0	0
Business Services	1	0	0
Total	39	25	18/72%

formation content for domestic manufacturers and firms. At the same time, our analysis also suggests that Arab speakers expect advertisements to conform to the rhetorical styles demanded by Arab culture, and that international advertisers are aware of these differences. This accounts for the greater use of features that typify Arab rhetoric.

As Table 4.3 shows, twenty-five of thirty-nine advertisements, or 64 percent, were placed by international, as opposed to domestic, companies.

MORES, NORMS, AND EFFECTIVE COMMUNICATIONS

Social roles, beliefs, and attitudes are all mirrored in the themes, copy, and illustrations used in advertisements. Whether the underlying concept of an advertising campaign depends on personal ideas or opinions, or the mores of a society, there are bound to be differences from one market to another. One simple means of assessing these differences, and variance in social roles, is to explore the way humans are portrayed in advertisements.

Are people portrayed alone, or in couples or groups? Are they engaged in some social activity, in motion, or are they shown in a posed, static illustration? Can their behaviors be related to a social, more intimate, or purely "on-the-job" relationship? Are they more interested in the task or the people they are with? Are the visuals "real" or invented, cartoon illustrations? The advertisements were categorized as follows:

Ad Theme Category	Definition
1. Interactional (social/recreational)	Males or females shown interacting on a social basis; friendship or involved in entertaining
2. Noninteractional (work, instruction)	Males or females shown involved or portrayed in occupational role or performing a task
3. No Theme	Males or females shown in background or foreground of the ad (e.g., an inset figure).

Fifteen of the forty advertisements (37.5 percent) contained actual (photographed) or simulated illustrations of human behavior. However, only one of the fifteen advertisements showed people interacting on a social basis; more often people are shown in noninteractional poses, or unengaged, that is, without a unifying "theme." Further, people are shown more in advertisements for products than for services, and those that portray men and women together are relatively rare. Only three advertisements showed men and women together in the same illustration. Most frequently, women and men are shown alone, or in same-sex pairs (the exception would be a woman and male child), and in static poses. Moreover, in most cases, men and women are shown in traditional occupational sex roles, possibly mirroring cultural preferences.

For women, these appear to be related to overall cultural traditionalism with regard to "hospitality," home maintenance, and supportive roles. For men, the preference appears also to be tied to traditional social roles: primarily more active, nonsupportive positions, with value placed on cooperative activities and tasks, usually related to some occupation. Women are shown presenting (and always physically in contact with) large home appliances, such as washers or gas ovens; sharing a meal with a child (with the suggestion that they are mother and child); or as sweet or cute (cartoon situation, a flower, the center of which is a human woman's face). Men are shown admiring pens, holding business meetings, and in the roles of pilot, chef, or cowboy (Marlboro cigarettes). Marlboro uses a well-known and highly successful Western image to good effect; the image works the world over.

None of the fifteen advertisements show an adult man and woman interacting on any basis, social or otherwise. The advertisements showing male and female are usually stock photos, transposed to the working frame without any referential clues to the relationship. That is, if the man and woman are "touching," it is the result of overlapping the photographs and not purposeful or thematic. Also, in cases where people are illustrated as engaged in a task, the women and children (two advertisements of the group) are portrayed looking directly at the audience, presenting the product to them, or involving them in the process by direct eye contact, while the men in almost all cases are shown looking at the object/task at hand, or looking obliquely at the audience (i.e., at a three-quarter turn).

Furthermore, it was rare to find persons of either sex actively engaged in any activity, or in motion. A preponderance of advertisements portrayed the human figure in an artificially posed, or static position. (This was true of advertisements in general, whether or not a human figure was included).

Although our interpretation of results can only be tentative, the pattern of findings supports previous research which has found that Arabs like some aspects of Arab culture more than others. Razzouk et al. (1988), Hashmi and Fouz (1989) and numerous other sources confirm that some aspects of the culture, such as strong family ties, religion (Islam), hospitality, personal relationships, and overall cultural traditionalism are liked more than others, or are intrinsic parts of Arab culture. Also, if we look beyond evidence of social interaction to other aspects of the advertisements, there is additional support for some of these ideas.

For example, the issue of religion does arise in circumstances where Islamic practices dictate that contractual obligations be sanctioned by God. Advertisements containing pledges, terms, and other contracts with regard to business or financial transactions therefore require the statement "In the Name of Allah" (found in advertisements for the Nile Bank and the National Bank of Development, showing simulated savings certificate, but not in advertisements for the Suez Central Bank, giving public notice of its financial statement for the previous year). By the same criteria, the Arabian credit card advertisement

Table 4.4 Frequency of Use of Languages in Advertisements (N=40)			
	Ads for Services	Ads for Products	Percent of Sample
All Arabic	2	10	30%
Some English (brand or company name, copy, package)	8	17	62.5%
All English	2	0	5%
All "Other" (Italian, French)	0	1	2.5%

looks rich, upscale, and inviting. A picture is worth a thousand and one words in the Middle East.

CONCLUSIONS AND IMPLICATIONS

As English spreads around the globe and international firms expand their presences in developing markets, opportunities for implementing intercultural, transnational marketing operations will be limited only by the mass media and distribution capabilities of the host country.

As Table 4.4 makes clear, 70 percent of the advertisements expected readers to know some English or other foreign language. Advertisers thus have choices to make with regard to the ways symbols, objects, and forms of communication. A key step in this process is the decision whether to standardize, or implement uniformly across markets, print media advertisements.

If, as our findings suggest, readers are evaluating the contents of Persian Gulf magazine advertisements based both on the attractiveness of the offers as well as on the writers' adherence to native speakers' culturally conditioned expectations regarding advertising and the way promotional messages are conveyed, we can say there is a trend toward globalization and a preference for non-Arab manufacture when prestige is at issue, or high-technology goods are offered. Nonetheless, on the basis of the data we concur with Onkvisit and Shaw that "until the world is ready to adopt a single language, a single currency and a single political ideology, it is premature to accept the standardized approach" (Onkvisit and Shaw, 1987).[3]

In sum, it may not be differences but attitudes toward those differences that play the largest role in determining the acceptance and effect of advertising standardization in cross-cultural contexts. To date there has been relatively little guidance with regard to the way advertising messages can best be conveyed in Mideast markets, and there is little information available that treats the marketing implications of message acceptability and how they should be judged. This study suggests the need for further research, and that this research might best be guided by Chittick's observation that "the Koran is the Word made Book, just as Christ is the Word made flesh. The images of the Koranic revelation are the pen and the tablet, ink, paper, letters, words, and verses" (Johnston, 1987). While sociolinguists and other scholars have recognized difficulties in specifying intentions and outcomes within as well as across cultures, qualitative analytic techniques, such as those applied to the challenges of assessing the role of languages in Middle Eastern advertising, may shed light on the most effective strategies for planning and decision making.

NOTES

Jane Frank teaches at the R. H. Smith School of Business at the University of Maryland, College Park, Maryland. She co-authored the chapter.

1. Various terms have been used more or less interchangeably to describe "international" marketing, other than that within the borders of one nation. Ralston (1988) defines "transnational direct marketing," as opposed to "single-country international direct," "multinational direct," or global direct, as "direct response advertising in any medium worldwide which is largely oblivious to differences in national markets for a product or service originating anywhere" (p. 32). For the most part, this term is sufficiently broad to describe direct-by-mail products and services sampled in this study, although the present authors suspect that the other terms may reasonably apply to individual examples.

2. Holbrook defines factual content as logical, objectively verifiable descriptions of tangible product features, in contrast to evaluative content, which might consist of emotional subjective impressions of intangible aspects of the product (1978, p. 547).

3. Following Onkvisit and Shaw (1987, p. 50), a standardized advertisement "is an advertisement which is used internationally with virtually no change in its theme, copy, or illustration, except for translations when needed."

REFERENCES

Banks, S. (1986). "Cross-national Analysis of Advertising Expenditures: 1968–1979." *Journal of Advertising Research* 26:2, 11–24.

Chittick, W. (1979). "The Words of the All-Merciful." *Parabola* 3, 18–47.

Fox, S. (1985). *The Mirror Makers: A History of American Advertising and Its Creators*. New York: Vintage Books.

Frank, J. (1988). "Mis-communication across Cultures: The Case of Marketing in Indian English." *World Englishes*, 7:1, pp. 25–36.

Gilly, M. (1988). "Sex Roles in Advertising: A Comparison of Television Advertisements in Australia, Mexico, and the United States." *Journal of Marketing* 52:2, 33–45.

Gumperz, J. (1982). *Discourse Strategies*. Cambridge: Cambridge University Press.

———. (1977). "Sociocultural Knowledge in Conversational Inference." In A. Saville-Troike (Ed.), *Linguistics and Anthropology*. Georgetown University Round Table on Languages and Linguistics, Washington, D.C.: Georgetown University Press, pp. 191–211.

Gumperz, J., and J. Cook-Gumperz (1981). "Ethnic Differences in Communicative Style." In Charles A. Ferguson and Shirley Brice Heath (Eds.), *Language in the USA*. Cambridge: Cambridge University Press, p. 430–435.

Hashemi, M., and K. Fouz (1989). "Marketing in the Islamic Context." Paper presented at the 8th Annual EMU Conference of Language and Communication for Business and Professions, Ann Arbor, MI.

Holbrook, M. (1978). "Beyond Attitude Structure: Toward the Informational Determinant of Attitude." *Journal of Marketing Research* 15:4, 545–556.

Johnston, B. (1987). "Parataxis in Arabic: Modification as a Model for Persuasion." *Studies in Language* 11:1, 85–98.

———. (1983). "Presentation as Proof: The Language of Arabic Rhetoric." *Anthropological Linguistics* 25: 47–60.

Madden, C. S., M. Cabvallero, and S. Masukubo (1986). "Analysis of Information Content in U.S. and Japanese Magazine Advertisements." *Journal of Advertising* 15:3, 38–45.

Onkvisit, S., and J. Shaw (1987). "Standardized International Advertising: A Review and Critical Evaluation of the Theoretical and Empirical Evidence." *Columbia Journal of World Business*, Fall Issue, 43–55.

Ralston, R. (1988). "Transnational Direct Marketing." *Direct Marketing* 50:12.

Razzouk, N., S. Johar, and F. Muna (1988). "Cultural Marginality and Ambivalence among Arabs." *Journal of International Consumer Marketing* 1:2, 101–120.

Resnik, A., and B. Stern (1977). "An Analysis of Information Content in Television Advertisements," *Journal of Advertising* 41:1, 50–53.

Rice, M., and Z. Lu, (1988). "A = 1F Content Analysis of Chinese Magazine Advertisements." *Journal of Advertising* 17:4, 41–48.

Sapir, D., and C. Crocker (Eds.), (1977). *Social Use of Metaphor: Essays on Anthropology of Rhetoric.* Philadelphia: University of Pennsylvania Press.

Scollon, R. and S.B.K. Scollon (1981). *Narrative, Literacy and Face in Interethnic Communication.* Norwood, N.J.: Ablex.

Smith, L. (Ed.) (1987). *Discourse across Cultures.* London: Prentice Hall.

Stern, B., D. Krugman, and A. Resnik (1981). "Magazine Advertising: An Analysis of Its Information Content." *Journal of Advertising* 21:2, 39–44.

Wind, Y. (1986). "The Myth of Globalization." *Journal of Consumer Marketing* 3, 23–26.

5

Religious and Social Context of Management in an Islamic Society

SCOPE OF THE STUDY

The role of culture seems to be crucial in explaining differences in management. Culture has a significant relationship with management policies and practices (Hofstede, 1993), and cultural values that enforce management are more likely to yield predictable behavior and enhanced performance (Schuler and Rogovsky, 1998). Studies on the particular case of the Middle East, specifically Morocco and Saudi Arabia, reinforce preexisting notions (Ali and Wahabi, 1995; Al-Aiban and Pearce, 1993).

Culture, defined as a way of life and internalization of a set of value systems that form the pattern of human relationships and behavior amongst individuals and their environment, has been shown to be a relatively stable component of countries (Hofstede, 1993). Hofstede's four cultural dimensions—power distance, individualist versus collectivist, uncertainty avoidance, and masculinity/femininity—have been tested in the case of the Middle Eastern Islamic states and have been found to exist in a wide spectrum ranging from collectivists to individualists, and masculinity versus femininity, among the Arab Islamic states. This partially explains, among the collectivist cultures, the existence of welfare bureaucratic states (Abu-Saad, 1998). Similar works on the non-Arab Turks confirms the significance of values in determining managerial styles, decision making, and conflict resolution mechanisms (Kozan and Ergin, 1998).

All these studies provide support for the proposition that culture is a significant explanatory factor for differences in management practices and policies, as well as for the proposition that the relationship between culture and management practices has validity.

The desire of many Muslims in Islamic countries to instill Islamic cultural values in the governance of their public and private affairs gives greater urgency for understanding the Islamization phenomenon.

One of the major goals of this chapter is to give more form and content to the process of Islamization of the Middle Eastern states. Islamization is seen here as a phenomenon whereby Islamic social scientists reject paradigms from the Western world and formulate their own, indigenous ones. This movement is seen as part of a struggle for disengagement from Western structures. Western social scientists and educators are thus put on notice that their paradigms, which they typically view as international reference models of intrinsic scientific worth, are viewed as part of the neoclassical postwar extension of the United States and Western Europe. The struggle is to reject them and to formulate "authentic indigenous models."

The major purpose here is to inform the reader of the existence of the Islamic world revolt against Western social science and also to elaborate on how Islamization, the process of this revolt, works. The chapter thus proposes to make readers aware and to warn them of the existence of this aspect of the Islamic revolt, and in addition to shed light on the specific case of the Middle East.

Islamization resulted in the creation by Iran of its own social science paradigms, or, less ambiguously, of local control of social science enterprises and the languages employed. The victory of the revolution brought about a reversal of power in which the *ulama* diminished the plausibility of Western modernization theory and practice as a universal phenomenon. (The ulama constitute the community of religious scholars in Islam.)

Prior to this, social science communications flowed from the centers of the disciplines to the peripheries of the Islamic world with little reverse flow, and with little communication and cooperation among the peripheries.

Muslim social scientists have indicted Western social science because it has justified colonialism or neocolonialism. They argue that on balance, Western social scientists have not contributed much to an understanding of Muslim problems—foreign experts have probably produced as much confusion as resolution. Islamization of the economy is viewed as a kind of revolt against the Western rationality of social movement and as a conflict with freedom of choice.

The earliest Western social scientists were historians bent on studying "primitive societies." Their studies were often "intended to reinforce the notion of the superiority of European culture and the importance of their civilizing mission." They provided the rationale for European and U.S. expansionism.

Universities imported a routinized social science that required no creative thinking. Muslims suffered in a "culture of silence," a culture that was an echo of the center. The center talked, and the Muslims listened. They absorbed the values, style of life, and the cultural myths of the West. Although modernization simulated the appearance of progress, it did not go beyond the mere reform of the structure; it maintained the state of dependence, and it brought a cultural invasion that deformed the society and reduced it to a species of caricature of the West. It gave many Muslims a Western vision of the world, at the expense of their originality.

Western-style capitalism, with its subsequent components, was offered as the universal development model, as change without revolution. The business elite was given special attention, as it was seen as the engine for growth and development. The challenge for an Islamic economy now is to seek an indigenous Islamic alternative.

ISLAMIC ALTERNATIVE

This section focuses mainly on Islamization in the strict sense, the process whereby Muslim social scientists reject the Western world's social sciences, like those discussed earlier, and create their own. The setting is the Middle East, where Islamization of life is being called for by an ever-increasing number of Muslims, from Turkey to Egypt. Proponents claim that "Islamic society" would purify society, promote cultural progress, provide universal justice, and exalt the word of God. Islamization, they maintain, is the sole remedy for the ills afflicting contemporary Muslim nations.

Opponents believe that an "Islamic society," unlike a "civil society," would be based on a narrow religious ideology and would, by definition, concentrate too much power in the hands of the *ulama* and their associates. Such a religious administration, they claim, would be inherently authoritarian. Thus, rather than providing a solution for the problems of the modern world, Islamic administration would pose a dangerous threat to the civil liberty of Muslims.

It is essential to understand the administration of such a society, both at the public and private level. The debate surrounding this issue presents a number of important questions. What does "Islamic management" mean? What are the ramifications of transforming the ideal of "Islamic management" into reality? Is an Islamic administration by definition a religious administration?

ISLAMIC MANAGEMENT

"Management" is defined as an act of administering and directing, ordering and shaping the elements necessary to perform a job. A manager sees to it that a job is accomplished, by utilizing the available resources and labor of others. For our purpose, we are concerned with the skills needed by a manager to accomplish this task.

In Islam, management is a derivative of leadership, which must be based on Islamic principles. The most fundamental Islamic principles are truth and justice.

Management style is shaped by a manager's values and personal characteristics, in addition to the values and character of those who work with him in an organization. Therefore, it may be assumed that context influences management style. The many contexts that have an impact on management include religion, language, politics, economics, and geography.

It is essential to understand the context in which a manager functions. In order to understand a manager's style one must also study the personal characteristics and value system of the individual.

Islam persists through a unique relationship between God, man, society, and divine love. This relationship should directly affect the workings of the various elements in an organization. To understand the organization of management and institutions in an Islamic system, it is important to acknowledge this relationship.

Islam encourages man to utilize to the fullest possible extent all the resources that God has created and entrusted to man for his use. Nonutilization of these resources for his benefits, or for the benefit of the society, is equal to wastefulness of these resources.

The Koran states six principles of Islamic management; each one is considered a fundamental pillar that a manager must follow (Koran). A manager must:

- Be a seeker of knowledge and searcher for the truth (Islam), surrender to the truth.
- Be a communicator, to provide for an effective system of communication.
- Have superior ethics and be able to attract pious employees.
- Have pure intentions and objectives, and total familiarity with Islamic values and its code of ethical conduct.
- Be a problem solver; a manager must have the qualities to enable him to solve complex problems.
- Have a fundamental belief in consultation and the process of deliberation in decision making.

AUTHORITY

Islam extends the principle of equality before the law, and equal protection and equal opportunity under the law to every member of the society. The underlying idea is to ensure maximum freedom of action for each individual, within the framework of the *shariah*.

The *shariah* consists of constitutive and regulative codes according to which individual Muslims and communities must conduct their affairs. The basic source of authority is the Koran. Compliance with the rules of the *shariah* is essential to the preservation of the community. The behavior of an individual is also constrained by adherence to the binding norms of the socioeconomic order, and through coercion by the collectivity. The rules cover the individual's relationships with other members of the society and with the collectivity (Al-Ashmawy, 1986).

So long as the decisions of the temporal authority conform to the principles of the *shariah* and are in the interest of the community, they must be obeyed. Self-interest, however, is not neglected in Islam. In fact, Islam considers it a primary factor for motivation, a necessity in any organization. A system of reward and punishment is fully developed in the principles of *shariah*.

OWNERSHIP

The first basic principle of ownership in Islam is that God is the ultimate owner of all property. In order that man may perform his duties and obligations, he has been given the privilege of position. The second principle of property establishes the right of the collectivity to the resources at man's disposal. Individuals are allowed to appropriate to themselves the products and profits resulting from the combination of their efforts, labor, and resources. The collectivity, however, does not lose its original rights either to the resources or to the products resulting from the individual's creative labor applied to these resources (Talegani, 1983).

LABOR AND OWNERSHIP

The relationship between labor and ownership is central in Islam, which recognizes two ways in which an individual can obtain rights to property: through his own creative labor, and through transfer, that is, inheritance of property rights from another individual who has gained title to the property or asset through his own labor. Work, therefore, is the basis of acquisition of rights to property.

CONTRACTS

The freedom to enter into contracts and the obligation to remain faithful to their stipulations is so emphasized in Islam that Muslims are distinguished by their faithfulness to the terms of contracts.

The contract in Islam is important, as an institution necessary for the satisfaction of legitimate human needs. The *shariah* itself is a social contract, a compact between God and man that imposes on man the duty of being faithful to his word and obligations.

In the *shariah*, the concepts of reward and punishment are linked to the fulfilment of obligations incurred under the stipulations of the contract. The *shariah* judges man not only for his material performance but also for the forthrightness of the intention with which he enters into every contract. This intention must consist of sincerity, truthfulness, and rigorous and loyal fulfilment of what one has consented to do. The Koran directs Muslims to reduce their contracts to writing and have witnesses to the conclusion of their agreements.

A body of rules constituting a general theory of contracts has been developed based on the *shariah*. It emphasizes contracts, such as sales, leases, hires, and partnerships. This body of rules establishes the principle that any agreement not specifically prohibited by *shariah* is valid and binding on parties and can be enforced by the courts, which are to treat the parties to a contract as complete equals.

LABOR AND PROFIT

The concept of labor in Islam is broad. Islam regards labor highly and considers it an indispensable dimension of faith itself. It considers idleness or spending time in pursuit of unproductive and nonbeneficial work as a manifestation of lack of faith. All able-bodied persons must work in order to earn their livings. No one who is mentally and physically able is allowed to become a liability of the family or the state through idleness and voluntary unemployment. The work that everyone is required to perform must be the best of which one is capable, but no work is considered inconsequential in terms of its rewards. Rewards must be provided as soon as the job is done—the concept of positive reinforcement.

The right to work must be guaranteed by the state, and businesses must provide every opportunity to work. Hence, based on its notion of individual choice and rights, Islam extends to the individual the right to choose the type of work he desires, but along with this freedom comes the social responsibility of individuals and businesses.

No line of work permissible by the *shariah* is considered demeaning by Islam. Since individuals are endowed with different abilities and talents, their productivity and interests differ. The rule is, from each according to his ability, to each according to his productivity. Profit is viewed positively, as a support for the community. Poverty is undesirable and reflection of social illness. Profits, however, must be generated in accordance with the laws of Islam.

Islam considers profits the lifeblood of private business, and that they must not be hampered. They must be invested within the community to improve its economic well-being. The need of the society, therefore, must be a consideration for the owner of capital.

The disposition of profits is subject to the rules of the *shariah* as well. After obligations are met, the remainder of profits belongs to the owner but must be used in accordance with the rules of the *shariah*, which forbids extravagance or waste. It cannot be used to harm others or to acquire political power to corrupt the society.

While Islam considers lawfully acquired, possessed, and disposed-of profits sacred and subject to the protection of the law, this profit is a trust, held on behalf of the community. Hence, one who misuses his profits may forfeit his right to wealth. Extravagance, waste, and general abuse of profits provide the basis for the community to classify him as a poor manager with weak character and leadership qualities, who, in addition to being immoral, is damaging the interests of the community. Such a person or business may lose the right to wealth or be allowed to use only a part of his or its property to meet basic needs. Such can provide the theoretical grounds for state intervention in the operation of a business, such as hostile takeovers or forced mergers.

The *shariah* provides a network of ethical and moral rules of behavior that cover the behavior of all participants in the market. It requires that its norms and rules be internalized personally and organizationally and adhered to by all participants before their entrance into the market. Demand in itself must not determine the price; price ought to be determined by observance of all Islamic codes of ethics. Not all demands are recognized as legitimate causes for production. Commodities must be produced with the needs and self-interest of the consumer in mind (Kahf, 1988).

The rules governing business must ensure just exchange. The freedom to make contracts and the obligation to fulfill them; consent of the parties to a transaction; full unrestricted access to the market by buyers and sellers; truth in transactions; provision of full information regarding quantity, quality, and prices at the time of market entry; and provision for full weights and measures—all are prescribed. On the other hand, fraud, cheating, withholding of information, monopolistic practices, coalitions and collaborations of all types among buyers or sellers, dumping, price fixing, and the bidding-up of prices without the intention to purchase are forbidden. The market must be a place for free exchange of fully informed and responsible men and women.

Although provisions are made for coercive and corrective action by authorities, the clear preference is for self-management of the market. All infrastructure necessary for the existence of a viable labor market is a responsibility of the state.

HUMAN RESOURCE MANAGEMENT IN THE PUBLIC SECTOR: SOME PRACTICAL ISSUES

One of the major problems facing the Islamic states today is a shortage of qualified and skilled white-collar and blue-collar industrial employees. In certain governments' agencies, the rate of unfilled positions reaches to 20 percent. Consequently, those who are employed carry a greater load of responsibility, to compensate for the shortages. This leads to further deterioration of employee morale and less efficiency. The inability of bureaucracies to attract the best and brightest, diminishes the organization's ability for self-renewal. Some of the main reasons for the shortages and the governments' inability to attract fully qualified personnel are the periodic purging of civil servants as politically considered untrustworthy; the retirement of highly experienced senior personnel without adequate replacement; voluntary departures, as well as death and disability; and the unattractiveness of government jobs, in some Middle Eastern countries, due to low salaries in comparison to the private sector. This is especially pronounced for individuals with highly specialized skills, such as technicians, engineers, physicians, and auditors, who prefer to work in the private sector. It is important to note that those who decide to stay in the government prefer large urban centers, which leads to greater centralization. The bulk of these civil servants prefer to work for certain prestigious government agencies that offer higher salaries and better employee benefits—the defense ministry, ministry of oil, ministry of foreign affairs, and ministry of commerce. This is normally at the expense of such ministries as education, agriculture, or transportation. Finally, many government agencies have made a deliberate policy decision to function with a bare minimum of personnel, partially as a result of depressed oil revenues in recent years.

IRAN'S POSTREVOLUTIONARY HUMAN RESOURCE NEEDS AND PROBLEMS

The postrevolutionary period has brought about a greater need for many new public services, which government agencies must address.

The postrevolutionary period has also been marked by war. War has had many indirect and direct impacts on human resource policies and on the allocation of manpower in the country.

Indirect Impact

Energy shortages and food rationing led to further expansion of the oil ministry in order to cope with regulative aspects and the processing of heating-oil and gasoline coupons throughout the country. The interior ministry, ministry of agriculture, and provincial agriculture ministries had to handle a massive demand for allocation of agriculture equipment to farmers. The ministry of transportation and the ministry of highway patrol faced severe difficulties in providing services to truckers. Lastly, the ministry of industries, whose responsibility is to ensure the smooth operation of factories and industrial plants, had major problems in providing energy needs.

Aside from food and energy, government agencies had to ensure that both basic and nonessential consumer goods were made available and distributed justly among the populace. For example, the allocation of sugar rations involved the ministry of commerce, the ministry of agriculture, local agriculture co-ops, and government nationalized banks, and it created a tremendous need for qualified personnel to implement the plans. Distribution of tea and household appliances, furnishings and food items, such as refrigerators, fans, carpets, heaters, cooking oil, detergents, soap, meat, and cheese, and other dairy products overwhelmed the respective government agencies and stretched thin their personnel. The overall social context of the work environment preoccupied employees and diverted their attention from their own main functions. This diversion was partly due to the fact that much time had to be devoted by salaried employees to ensuring that they obtained coupons themselves and purchased their own necessities before stores ran out of stock. The distribution of construction materials, such as iron bars, cement, bricks, tiles, pipes, etc., accounted for a large amount of effort by the ministries of commerce, industries, budget and planning, and housing and urban planning, as well as by provincial and city governments. Any new product that was rationed created a new responsibility for several government agencies, which required additional human resources. It is important to note that the private sector handles the largest portion of distribution channels.

Direct Impact

In addition to the indirect involvement of the public sector on the allocations of the nation's human resources, the direct consequences of the eight-year Iran-Iraq War deserve attention.

Many of the resources of the frontline provinces and government agencies responsible for their welfare were directly devoted to the war effort. For example, the ministry of transportation, ministry of health and human services, and the agriculture ministry allocated a substantial portion of their human resources to alleviate problems that resulted from Iraqi attacks. The reconstruction of war-damaged areas took a large toll on those ministries. Given the fact that no new employees were added to these organizations, that work naturally diverted the energy of the employees from their routine job descriptions. In addition, the government became heavily involved in an intricate array of business decisions. For example, the law required companies to get permission for a range of decisions, such as changing prices on commodities, importing raw materials, hiring and firing employees, etc. The law established subjective criteria for many of these decisions, so bureaucrats have a great deal of discretion in how to apply the rules.

Intricate relations between business and government, in fact, appears to be the norm throughout the Middle East. Major Middle Eastern firms all have strong government connections to reduce risk. Until recently, the ties between government and industry in the Middle East have been a centerpiece of the region's economic program. Even today there are groups whose greatest assets appear to include access to high government officials. Because bureaucrats are so involved with companies, managers must be prepared to deal with government and its agencies. It is important to note that, for example, in Iran, by 1982, nearly 15 percent of all manufacturing enterprises with ten or more workers, employing about 70 percent of the manufacturing workforce, were under public management (*Statistical Yearbook*, 1983).

Another major factor contributing to manpower problems in the postrevolutionary period has been rapid population growth. The country has witnessed a 3.5 percent population growth, one of the highest birthrates in the world. This growth is putting pressure on the educational and health resources of the country. In addition, the country is faced with major housing shortages, especially in the urban areas. Given the fact that the Islamic Republic's constitution obliges the state to provide such services for the citizenry, the role of government is vital.

INTEGRATION OF CONTEXT AND MANAGEMENT PRACTICES

That the techniques of Islamic management do not stand alone, but rather require supporting cultural and environmental frameworks to be effective, seems to be in little doubt (Ali, 1988). The important question, however, is how and to what extent the supporting framework fosters the development of, or reinforces, existing management practices in Islamic organizations.

The idea of simultaneous causality must be applied in order to attempt to comprehend the complexity of the relationships between the social context and Islamic management practices, grasp the complex reality that underlines Islamic organizational administration. Such conceptual methodology has not been widely attempted by management scholars in the field of Islamic management.

It seems likely that each management practice exists within a supportive system of interlocking elements from the social context (Islam, revolution, or war) as well as from other contexts that are beyond the scope of this chapter—linguistic, economic, etc. In Islamic management, a mutual reinforcing relationship is, however, encouraged. For example, the need to be part of a context or group will motivate an individual to seek out and enter a group and to do whatever is necessary to maintain membership in that group. A natural outcome of this state of affairs is the lack of need on the part of the organization to create massive external control mechanisms to ensure the employee does what he or she was hired to do. The worker controls his or her own behavior to satisfy the need for contextualism at that moment in time. Indeed, if the organization tried to impose external control mechanisms in such situations they would alienate workers, for the workers would feel that they were being viewed with suspicion and were considered outsiders to the group. Product sabotage, lower productivity, and higher absenteeism would likely result.

Over the centuries, Muslims have adopted other systems of management. The brief sketch presented here should make it clear that Islam proposes a viable system for the creation of a modern society and management.

OBSERVATIONS ON ISLAMIZATION

Muslims today are looking toward a future that holds Islamic promises, and they are prepared to solve their problems with Islamic solutions, alternatives, and options. This preoccupation with Islam is a quest for indigenization. With Muslims expressing themselves in Islamic rationale, Islam is coming to terms with modernity and with itself in this new historical juncture. It has proved itself as a most effective modern instrument of change. Gone are the days of the Western view of Islam as a postclassical civilization.

With its revitalization, Islam is bringing the exterior world into alignment with its value system. As long as Islam has this power of constructing itself as a political force, and as long as it can generate answers in terms of moral values, it can and will remain a major, viable force.

REFERENCES

Abu-Saad, I. (1998). "Individualism and Islamic Work Beliefs." *Journal of Cross-Cultural Psychology* 29:2.

Al-Aiban, K. M., and J. L. Pearce (1993). "The Influence of Values on Management Practices: A Test in Saudi Arabia and the United States." *International Studies of Management and Organization* 23: 3.

Al-Ashmawy, S. (1986). "Islamic Government." *Middle East Review* (Spring).

Ali, A. (1988). "A Cross-National Perspective of Managerial Work Value Systems." In *Advances in International Comparative Management,* vol. 3. Greenwich, Conn.: JAI Press.

Ali, A., and R. Wahabi (1995). "Managerial Value Systems in Morocco: Management and Its Environment in the Arab World." *International Studies of Management and Organization* 25:3.

Barakat, H. (1993). *The Arab World: Society, Culture, and the State*. Berkeley: University of California Press.

Gareau, F. (1986). "The Third World Revolution against First World Social Science." *International Journal of Comparative Sociology*, 27.

Hofstede, G. (1993). "Cultural Constraints in Management Theories." *Academy of Management Executive* 7:1, 81–94.

———. (1980). *Cultures Consequences: International Differences in Work-Related Values*. Beverly Hills, Calif.: Sage.

Iran: Statistical Yearbook (1983). Tehran: Statistical Center of Iran.

Iran Times, February 12–April 15, 1998.

Kahf, M. (1981). "A Contribution to the Theory of Consumer Behavior in Islamic Society." In K. Ahmad (Ed.), *Studies in Islamic Economics*. Jeddah, Saudi Arabia: International Center for Research on Islamic Economics, King Abdul-Aziz University; Leicester, U.K.: Islamic Foundation.

Koran, *Sura* [chapter] Tah, *Ayat* [verse] 25–34.

Kozan, M. K., and C. Ergin (1998). "Preference of Third Party Help in Conflict Management in the United States and Turkey: An Experimental Study." *Journal of Cross-Cultural Psychology*, 29:4.

Schuler, R., and N. Rogovsky (1998). "Understanding Compensation Practice Variations across Firms: The Impact of National Culture." *Journal of International Business Studies* 29:1.

Shackleton, V. J., and A. Ali (1990). "Work Related Values of Managers: A Test of Hofstede Model." *Journal of Cross-Cultural Psychology* 21.

Talegani, S. M. (1983). *Islam and Ownership*. Tehran: Foundation of Islamic Thought.

6

Interest-Free Banking: Banking on Islam

In Muslim countries, where Islamic law forbids payment of interest, financial markets are limited by religious variables. Although some countries have attempted to circumvent these laws, the emergence of "Islamic banks" may provide a solution to the problems of poverty and underdevelopment, as discussed in this chapter. Continuing growth of commerce throughout the world and the need for more varied forms of lending and enticements to save or invest have led to the international banking industry we know today.

This same rationale has led to the development of financial markets in less-developed countries. It is the development of such markets and their contribution to the development and modernization of their respective countries that are the subjects of this chapter.

INTRODUCTION

The present state of Islamic banking represents a phase that started almost four decades ago in a number of countries around the world with different innovating styles, motivations, and incentives. In the early 1960s, countries such as Algeria and Egypt attempted to establish Islamic banks. None existed long enough to produce results. See Table 6.1.

Islamic banks or financial institutions are defined here as those that

Table 6.1 Islamic Banks and Financial Institutions	
Region	Number of Banks/Financial Institutions
South Asia	50
Africa	35
Southeast Asia	30
Middle East	43
Europe/North America	8

Source: Extrapolated and extracted from Stephen Timewell, *The Banker*, February 1998.

display one or both of the following characteristics: they were established initially to operate within Islamic *shariah* and restrict their activities to its bond; and they have been charged by their national legislatures to shift from conventional to Islamic banking.

Banking, in its basic form, is the international function between those that have money (individuals and institutional savers/investors) and those that need money, (individuals and institutions organized to produce items of value to a consuming public, and borrowers). In order for borrowers to be allowed to use the monies of the saver/investor, they must pay rent, or in banking terms, interest.

This borrowing/lending (investing) activity is a time-honored function that has taken many forms throughout the history of commerce. As commercial activities grew, the need for a convenient medium of exchange grew, thus the advent of "money." As commercial activities became more widespread, the distance between those that needed monies—the borrowers—and those that had monies—the savers/investors—became larger. Thus there developed a need for an intermediary to bring these two together. Hence the emergence of banking as we know it. The continuing growth of commerce throughout the world and the need for more varied forms of lending and enticements to save and invest have led to the international banking industry we know today. This same rationale has led to the development of financial markets in less-developed countries.

Although a few studies have been conducted on the contribution of financial markets in developing countries to the development process, the existing literature concentrates on the financial markets in Southeast Asia. The first part of the chapter will discuss two theories that will demonstrate to the reader the importance of financial markets in the development process. Research on Saudi Arabia follows, as a case in point. The next section of the chapter discusses the development of societies and Islam, the modernization process, and its effects on society. The third section discusses the development of financial markets and their importance to the modernization process. The fourth section of the chapter presents an innovative development program describing a new type of banker, the Islamic interest-free bank. The final section summarizes the discussion and makes some concluding remarks.

SOCIETAL DEVELOPMENT, ISLAM, AND MODERNIZATION

Societal Values, Religion, and Interest

Societal values are those norms, mores, and guidelines or policies that bind a group of people into a cooperative whole or "society," where individual activities are directed either for the good of the society—or at least not against the good of the society. As long as the value of each societal member is that of only one of a small group of individuals, each is in conflict with the values of the society as a whole. In such a case, dissident groups will break off and form separate entities incorporating their own value systems. These two societies now have a choice of existing separately without any interaction, or of finding a method of interaction that is mutually acceptable. Since there usually is a set of common values between the societies, and cooperation usually leads to improvement of both, as explained in classical trade theories, the latter is most often the chosen alternative. Indeed, one would be hard pressed to locate a society in today's world that does not interact in some way with other societies.

For most societies today, the payment of interest is in line with its value system. This stems from the religious value that if you borrow from your neighbor, you should repay him with value greater than that which you deprived him of, thus enriching your neighbor. This implies that "money has value." Herein develops a conflict between societies.

With the establishment of Islam as the dominant organizing principle of the Orient in the sixth century A.D., the societal norm of paying interest on borrowed money came under fire. In Islamic *shariah* law, "money" is only a means of facilitating exchange and has no value in and of itself. Therefore, the payment of interest from the borrowing of money is not necessary. The *shariah* prohibits the payment of interest on borrowed money.

During most of the history of Islamic societies and nations, their economies have been agrarian and rural. The need for banking has been minimal; therefore, coexistence with societies that allowed payment of interest on borrowed money was not difficult, though interactions were kept at a minimum. This changed abruptly in the 1970s. Most of the Islamic nations were rich in petroleum, a commodity needed by Western, interest-paying nations. Sales of this commodity brought inconceivable amounts of money into the Islamic states. Suddenly, these states became the world's largest savers/investors. While the need for consumption tends strongly to modernize a society and bring it closer to other nations in the world, this modernization takes time. In the meantime, there was the question of what to do with the excess cash in the coffers.

Western thinking would lead one to offer to lend the excess cash at interest to those with an immediate need for consumption. In Islam, however, this is not allowed. This precipitated Islamic interest-free banking.

Modernization and Islamic Societies

A second event in the late 1970s further brought to light the need for a customized banking system. With the ascension of the Ayatollah Khomeini to the societal leadership of Iran, there was a resurgence of traditional Islamic values and laws. This created a major conflict. On the one hand was the need and means for modernizing Islamic nations, while on the other hand was the return to traditional values.

As Wilbert Moore suggests in his *World Modernization*, modernization may appropriately be described as a "rationalization" of the way life and activities are organized. Moore writes that this process is limited by three conditions: the logical limit—the criteria used in choosing the procedures used to reach a stated goal or objective; the biopsychological limit—the human tendencies toward emotion, ethical convictions, and sentiment; and the sociological limit—the form of legitimate power that coordinates the differentiated units within the society. These three limits create a restraining force on the evolution of a rational or modern society.

The rationales for certain beliefs, practices, and sources of legitimate power have traditional roots. Tradition is especially important, in its effect on the logical limit. In most societies, rules are followed, beliefs are accepted, and authority is obeyed because that is the way life has always been organized. Older generations teach younger generations until the belief or rule loses its origin and becomes so integrated that it simply "exists." These traditionalized beliefs and practices are the components of the logical limit and are not always based on "rational" thought. Often, traditional beliefs have their orientation in the supernatural, whether religion or magic. At times, even leaders of the state have been worshiped, as though they were beings of a higher order. This traditional thinking becomes a hindrance to the modernization of a society.

It seems quite logical that the elements of the biopsychological limit would also hinder the rationalization or modernization process. Emotions such as love, hate, and religious convictions have led many people to behave irrationally. Men and women have been known to kill for love or hate, and certain religious groups have been prone to terrorism in the name of their respective religions.

Irrational behavior is not limited to the governed; it also applies to the governors. Ultimate authority is derived from those biopsychological values that form the criteria of the sociological limit. Therefore, since ultimate authority drives its legitimacy from nonrational beliefs and values, it also has a restraining effect on the rationalization process.

In light of such limits, it seems that the hope for a rational society is rather dim, or at best, that it will be a slow process. Since the Age of Reason (Moore, 1979), rational philosophers such as Plato, Aristotle, and Hobbes, along with such scientists as Galileo and Newton, have thought and written objectively of social and universal order. Although it has been established that man is not completely rational by nature, the conceptions and theories born during the Age of Reason kindled the quest for a rational society.

The desire for an orderly society led people to use fact and logic in choosing behavior that will propel the society toward the achievement of various goals. But as man took charge of his own destiny, he shifted away from adapting to his environment and instead began to adapt the environment to himself, providing more order in his existence. Environment adaptation brought about the development of technology needed to order the natural elements. This movement toward increasing rationalization is fundamental to the modernization process.

As the use of technology in the modernization process made societies more productive and efficient, trade began. With the end of serfdom and feudal property systems, labor markets and enlarged capital markets arose. Commercialization became more complex, which gave rise to a monetized market system. This monetization and consequent development of societal economics was (and still is) the crucial mechanism for the rationalization of exchange and distribution.

FINANCIAL MARKETS AND THE DEVELOPING NATIONS

In subsistence economies, financial markets are almost nonexistent. Investors and savers tend to be identical, and most private investment depends on prior self-saving. Fiscal policies to capture private savings and reliance on heavy government expenditure have been the major components of the economic development process in these countries.

Financial markets in even more sophisticated less-developed countries (LDCs) are underdeveloped, inefficient, and dominated by commercial banking systems. The primary financial assets are bank deposits. Other assets, such as bonds, are held mainly by the financial institutions and not by the saving public. There is little or no domestic securities market, and interest rates are determined by the government. Since government investment plays such a large role in LDC economies, there is usually a large budget deficit, which is financed by borrowing from the central bank, commercial banks, or foreign markets (Coats and Khatkhate, 1984). Presently Middle Eastern states run an average budget deficit of 3 to 5 percent of gross domestic product.

If long-term growth and development is the objective, the monetary policies of LDCs should be directed toward the eradication of inefficiencies in their financial sectors. The role of money must be viewed in developing countries as that of a distribution agent, through which the unused savings of one sector in the economy is channeled to another sector, where they are put to more efficient use. This developmental role of money can be described by two developmental monetary theories: the *Shaw-McKinnon framework*, and the *flow-of-funds approach*.

The Shaw-McKinnon framework stipulates that more rapid economic growth requires more investment and that this implies the need for a more efficient use of savings. When other financial assets are nonexistent, the only use of savings is self-investment by lending activities in the very limited neighborhood market. As a result, deserving high-yield investments are never made, because the funds flow into less productive, more conservative hands. This unfortunate fact makes it clear that what is lacking is an efficient channel that would transmit surplus resources to projects in greater need of them.

The Shaw-McKinnon theory was conceived when it became apparent that "low interest rate" policies, intended to encourage investment and economic growth, were actually retarding the development of the financial markets and impeding efficient allocation of surplus resources. The framework suggests raising the real rate of return on money and other financial assets in the organized sectors of the economy to the marginal return on investment, to encourage high saving rates (Coats and Khatkhate, p. 336).

Shaw-McKinnon also implies a complementary relationship between real money balances and capital formation, rather than the neoclassical view of money and capital as competing elements (Coats and Khatkhate, p. 338). For example, since monetary assets form the largest part of community savings in LDCs, when assets are released and transmitted into investment through financial intermediaries (savings), the rate of capital investment (in machinery and equipment) becomes higher. Therefore, it would be evident that money and capital are complementary to each other; by extension, upward adjustment of the return on money balances would encourage more surplus earnings into investment through financial intermediaries.

The flow-of-funds approach applies to economies whose financial sectors cannot be considered repressed but are simply underdeveloped, like the economies in general. This theory of developmental monetary policy sharpens the focus on the need to increase aggregate investment by directing the flow of savings from surplus to deficit sectors. This can be seen more clearly if the economy is divided into three primary units (Coats and Khatkhate, p. 238). The first is the household sector, which is made up of individuals, private trusts, and small business. The second is the corporate sector, and the third is the government, which includes all public enterprises. The evidence indicates that in LDCs the household sector tends to be a "surplus spending" sector. The corporate and government sectors are predominantly "deficit spending" units (Coats, p. 239). If growth is to occur, it is essential that the resources saved in surplus units be put to their most productive use and that the amount of these surpluses be increased. Since fulfillment of these objectives requires more attractive financial assets to draw funds from the surplus sector, policies must be instituted to supply the desired assets.

The focus of the Shaw-McKinnon theory is on increasing the flow of funds from the surplus sector into the financial institutions and on increasing the level of the money balances. It is primarily on this point that the two theories differ. The objective of the flow-of-funds approach is not simply to increase aggregate savings but to promote transferable savings by increasing the ratio of differentiated financial assets to total savings.

Empirical evidence indicates that the elasticity of demand for money is inversely related to the stage of development of money and capital markets (Coats and Khatkhate, p. 236). In other words, where the main asset of an economy's financial sector is bank deposits, money is sought after primarily as a storehouse of wealth. As financial markets become better organized, the range of assets offered widens to include bonds and shares. Factors such as risk aversion and liquidity need tend to heighten the desire for a differentiated package of investment assets. Therefore, as development increases, financial assets other than money need to be created to preclude savers from investing excessively in their own activities, wasting the productive power of their surplus resources.

The main thrust of both the Shaw-McKinnon and the flow-of-funds approaches is that the role of the financial markets in developing countries is to transfer savings from surplus to deficit sectors and to allocate the resources efficiently. In financially repressed economies, the general tenets of the Shaw-McKinnon theory are applicable. As financial markets evolve, the insights of the flow-of-funds approach should be heeded.

Empirical research has established that money in the Islamic countries of the Middle East is not a medium of investment but is held only for transactions purposes ("Free the Markets," 1983). According to both the Shaw-McKinnon and the flow-of-funds approaches, this evidence indicates that there is no proper channel of savings, that money and capital are still viewed as competing elements. An IMF study completed in 1980 by Andrew Crockett and Owen Evans discovered that money in circulation plus time and demand deposits

(M1 and M2) are determined largely by income levels in these countries ("Free the Markets," p. 41). Tests were conducted to see if such variables as the rate of inflation deterred the desire to hold money for transactions purposes, but in general, the results were negative ("Free the Markets," p. 43).

It seems that banks in Middle Eastern countries provide services to the public in currency exchange and trade finance but do little in the way of channeling surplus funds into productive sectors. In addition, these economies have a much lower proportion of time and savings deposits of national income (M2/Y) than developed economies. This is precisely what the Shaw-McKinnon theory terms "financial repression" (Coats and Khatkhate, 1984). Therefore, because money is not supplied for investment purposes, banks are not able to fulfill their roles as channels of finance. This consequently leads to a thin resource base for the commercial banks.

ISLAMIC INTEREST-FREE BANKING

The previous discussion points out the primary issue of conflict in the development of the banking systems in Islamic countries. On one hand, Islamic economies hold that "money" has no value in and of itself. Islamic law further prohibits the payment of interest, or *riba*. Therefore, for the income earner, there is no apparent reason for using a bank, with the possible exception of security from burglary; cash can be stored as easily and more conveniently at home. On the other hand, the modernization of Islamic nations requires the use of funds in specific locations, usually remote from the income earner.

As stated earlier, the basic function of a bank is to act as the intermediary in channeling funds that are not in use today in one sector (the income earners) to another sector (the modernization efforts), where they are needed today. The challenge is to devise a system that promotes this activity while still obeying *shariah* law.

Modern Islamic banking centers around the Western concept of money not as simply a "bill of exchange" but as a factor of production having value in itself. Islam faults Western banking practices on four accounts: they do not take into account social welfare considerations of the society; they legitimize and perpetuate wealth and income inequalities; those with money can direct resources into production and services harmful to society; and money market forces are blind and indiscriminate.

The fundamentalists, Islamists or centralists, who aspire to restore Islam to its original purity and escape from alien influences, have attempted to prove the suitability and adaptability of the Islamic doctrine of economics to the needs of modern times. They have developed a concept of interest-free banking (Ajami, Khambata, and Kavoossi, 1992).

The sponsors of those banks argue that the Islamic banks are not much different from the familiar Western banks that prevail in Islamic countries. The only difference is that Islamic banks are not based on fixed rates of interest on loans or deposits, which, from their point of view, are usurious under the *shariah*. Western banks not only deal in money but invest in agriculture, commercial, and industrial and human projects that provide for the needs of the society. Islamic banks can deal and invest in such projects but without the use of *riba*. The abolition of *riba* is based on two premises: first, Islam believes that its followers should not accumulate wealth through money lending; second, Islam believes in accumulation of wealth through productive activities as opposed to idle usury (Esposito, 1980).

Islamic interest-free banking offers alternatives to the undesirable aspects of modern Western banking. Allocation of resources is determined by free market needs, modified by social and moral considerations should they conflict with the goals of the society. The goals of the society, in accordance with Islam, are twofold: consumers (investors) may not vote for something (through allocation of financial resources) socially undesirable; the objective of financial resource allocation is not maximizing the utility of the factors of production (capital) but fulfillment of the "needs" of the society. Investments are to be determined by societal needs and are guided by the Islamic principles of: money as worthless in itself but merely a means of exchange and measure of value; success as not entailing acquisition of greater and greater material wealth (money); and God as the sole arbiter, with the right to lay down the mode of resource allocation and utilization. By offering these ideals as the basis for the banking system, income earners can be induced to provide the savings needed for investment.

Broadly speaking, Islamic banks maintain three types of accounts: nonprofit accounts with small minimum deposits, from which withdrawals can be made at any time; profit-sharing deposit accounts, with a modest minimum balance, from which withdrawals can be made periodically, with some restrictions; and social service funds, consisting primarily of gifts, from which withdrawals are made in case of emergency. More recently there have emerged two types of institutions to satisfy market niches: commercial/consumer banking, and institutional/investment banking.

As mentioned above, "interest" as a form of payment for use of capital funds is prohibited. The Koran prohibits "interest" (*riba*) numerous times. As interest is prohibited for all purposes and in all its forms as far as Islamic doctrine is concerned, one must look elsewhere for a system consistent with Islam. A permissible form of business relationship between those who provide capital funds and those who use it can be found in Islamic literature. Reallocation of capital on the basis of sharing in any profit or loss is permissible, provided the use of capital is in line with the goals of society. This argument provides the fundamental basis for the Iranian nationalization of banks and financial institutions, including limiting lending to only 4 percent service charges paid to banks. This took place at a time when rampant inflation of up to 50 percent tested the limits of the newly established nationalized Islamic interest-free banks.

Islamic banking has developed seven instruments for allocating funds as needed. These are listed and described in Table 6.2. In many respects they are similar to certain Western banking practices and techniques. For example, *murabaha* is almost identical to the institution of a merchant middleman or the Japanese general trading company (*Sogo Sosha*). *Mudaraba* is similar to a limited partnership. In all of these instruments is the belief that the risks and rewards should be shared by all three parties to the transaction: the user of the capital (the borrower), the bank, and the supplier of the capital (the income earner). *Murabaha* is perhaps the most controversial instrument. Fundamentalists argue that, in practice, there is no difference between the use of a markup and interest. Supporters of the arrangement have no objection, since there is no penalty for late payment. Once the markup is established, the payment is fixed. Also, since the bank takes title, it performs a service and is entitled to be compensated for its efforts.

The first major project of this type was started in Dubai in March 1975, after long study and investigation. Between 1975 and 1983, new Islamic banks were established primarily in the Middle Eastern countries such as Iran, Egypt, Saudi Arabia, Kuwait, Sudan, Bahrain, Pakistan, the United Arab Emirates, and Jordan. Since 1983, Islamic banks have been established throughout much of the world. Banks

Table 6.2 Techniques Used in Islamic Interest Free Banking	
Murabaha	The Islamic bank purchases, in its own name, goods that an importer or trader wants and then sells them to him at an agreed markup. This technique is used for trade financing, but because the bank takes title to the goods and is therefore engaged in buying and selling, its profit drives from a real service that entails a certain-albeit minimal-risk and is thus seen as legitimate. Simply advancing the money to the client at a fixed interest rate would not be legitimate.
Mudaraba	An Islamic bank lends money to a client-to finance a factory, for example-in return for which the bank will get a specified percentage of the factory's net profit every year for a designated period. Should the factory lose money, the bank, its depositors, and the borrower all jointly absorb the losses, thereby putting into practice the pivotal Islamic principle that the providers and users of capital should share risks and rewards.
Mugarada	This novel technique allows a bank to float what are effectively Islamic bonds to finance a specific project. Investors who buy *mugarada* bonds take a share of the profits of the project being financed but also share the risk of unexpectedly low profits, or even losses. They have no say in the management of the project but act as nonvoting shareholders.
Musharaka	The bank enters into a partnership with a client in which both share the equity capital-and perhaps even the management-of a project or deal, and both share in the profits or losses, according to their equity shareholding.
Ijara-Ijara Wa Iktina	Equivalent to the leasing and installment-loan, or hire-purchase, practices that put millions of drivers on the road each year, these techniques as applied by Islamic banks include the requirement that the leased items be used productively and in ways permitted by Islamic law.
Salam	A buyer pays in advance for a specific quantity and quality of a commodity, deliverable on a specific date, at an agreed price. This financing technique, similar to a future or forward-purchase contract, is particularly applicable to seasonal agricultural purchases, but it can also be used to buy other goods in cases where the seller needs working capital before he can deliver.

offering Islamic banking services are located in Turkey, Malaysia, Bangladesh, Tunisia, Denmark, Great Britain, Guinea, Senegal, Switzerland, Luxembourg, and India (*Wall Street Journal*, 1996). By 1987 there were over a hundred Islamic banking institutions in existence. These institutions exist successfully side by side with Western banking institutions in most countries. Only Iran and Pakistan have required all banks in their territory to be interest free. Islamic banking companies like Al Baraka and Dar Al Islami are actively establishing new institutions throughout the world as well as developing new financial investments with which to interact with Western-style financial institutions (Khouri, 1987).

Of the nearly 170 banks and financial institutions now in existence, eighty-eight are considered to operate within the *shariah*; the remainder are government-legislated organizations, which claim to adhere to the *shariah* as well ("Islamic Banks," 1997). With total assets exceeding $170 billion and employing 271,000 people, these banks have a heavy concentration in the Middle East (where approximately forty of the total institutions are situated), followed by South Asia. Ten of the twenty-four Islamic banks in the Persian Gulf region are in Iran. Over the past several years, the number of Islamic banks and financial institutions have been growing at more than 15 percent a year, with a financial market currently estimated at $70 billion ("Islamic Banking Gains Momentum," 1988). Therefore it is not surprising to see that many Western firms, including Chase Manhattan, Citicorp, Bankers Trust, Republic New York, and Goldman Sachs have adhered to Islamic requirements in several Middle Eastern countries ("Western Banks, Taking 1st Steps," 1997). In 1996 Citicorp initiated the CitiIslamic Investment Bank (CIIB) in Bahrain with a capital of $20 million. It is the first Western bank to create a purely Islamic bank with a board that monitors its compliance with the *shariah*, except for a failed attempt by German banks in Algeria in 1964.

The process of establishing Islamic banking appears to be well entrenched, at least in Pakistan and the Islamic Republic of Iran. It raises two questions. Does such a system make sense? Can it work in a modern setting? The first of these questions was examined above, showing that it is indeed possible to rationalize the profit-and-loss sharing system. With respect to the second question, however, because the experience with an economywide profit-and-loss sharing system is relatively recent, it is not possible to state with confidence that such a system functions as well or better than the traditional banking system. The need for empirical analysis of this system gives rise to topics for future research.

These banks have been showing what could be considered responsible profitability. The Jordan Islamic Bank for Finance and Investment has earned a gross average return on its deposits and savings of between 2.74 percent and 8 percent since 1980, depending on the type of deposit, as described earlier. The Faisal Islamic Bank of Egypt has recorded a 16.52 percent return on capital and has paid a 9 percent return on deposits in investment accounts. The Al Baraka Islamic Bank, started in 1984 to create a secondary market for Islamic financial instruments, has distributed returns to its depositors of 8.44 percent (Khouri, p. 15).

It is tempting to use standard financial analysis techniques to analyze the interest-free banks and compare them to Western-style banks. For several reasons, this is inappropriate and would lead to misleading conclusions. Since Islamic investments are not based on the principle of earning interest, profitability ratios, such as return on primary capital, return on earning assets, and return investments, are not applicable. Concepts such as "primary capital" and "earning assets" do not exist in interest-free banking. Investments in the interest-free instruments are not equivalent to bonds or earning assets but are closer to shares in limited partnership ventures. In interest-free banking, "returns" are based on profit sharing, not repayment schedules. Equally, capital does not exist per se in Islamic banking. Capital is supplied by investors as long-term deposits or "gifts," and have a shared-ownership characteristic. In addition, there is no tax on earnings from the interest-free investments, thus making comparisons inappropriate. Take, for example, an Islamic investment that returns 2.74 percent; should this be grossed up using the 48 percent corporate tax rate, or, since the investment has a profit-sharing character, should it be grossed up at the personal tax rate? Finally, Islamic banks are not in business only to make a profit; they are in business for the good of the society, as dictated in *shariah* law. As such, they make investments such as *"qard hassan,"* or social purpose, loans to the poor and needy, at no charge. This is unique to Islamic banking and distorts their profit picture.

In keeping with the flow-of-funds approach, the Middle Eastern banking sector has been making progress toward maturity by diversifying and improving its services. Though small by international standards (the entire interest-free banking industry has only $170 billion in deposits), interest-free banking has been quite aggressive in establishing its legitimacy and viability in Islamic societies. New and innovative services are being developed rapidly. The Kuwait Finance House (KFH), one of the largest interest-free banks, has been offering an instrument similar to a real estate limited partnership. Investors purchase "certificates," effectively shares, in a real estate portfolio. They then share in the rental income from the properties. Since this income can be gauged reasonably well in advance, these instruments effectively offer their participants an "expected rate of return" of 6.5 percent to 8 percent (Khouri, p. 16). A similar innovation offers buyers the right to purchase apartments and homes on a ten-year mortgage arrangement. As in Western banking, these mortgages are on a participation basis with other local savings institutions. The Saudi Monetary Agency (SAMA) has been attempting to speed up the check-clearing process, and all banks have installed computers to handle their internal processing needs. In 1984, the Saudi American Bank—a Citibank affiliate—was the first bank to introduce automatic teller machines ("Banking Sector," 1984).

For corporate borrowers, services have improved tremendously. A group of dollar and riyal–denominated loans set up for a number of heavy-industry companies have given banks opportunities to prove that they can underwrite complex, medium-term credits ("SAMA Listings," p. 98). Although rich investors must still look outside the kingdom for sophisticated portfolio management, in-house training programs have been established to upgrade the skills of the nationals. In addition, Saudi banks have recently invested a large amount of money and effort into building head offices and opening new branches. This has been done to increase visibility, and developments indicate that a majority of the population is now making use of bank services ("SAMA Listings," p. 97).

SAMA has also demonstrated its commitment to the modernization of capital markets, by controlling money exchangers and instituting a ban on share dealing by brokerage companies and other nonbank financial institutions. SAMA has also introduced the kingdom's first treasury bill–type system, known as the Bankers Security Deposit Account (BSDA). This is innovative because it is the first time that the Saudi government has openly involved itself in paying interest to local lenders.

The Arab Investment Company (TAIC) likes to see itself as the Arab twin of the International Finance Corporation, a World Bank agency that specializes in private-sector development. New investments since 1953 include Jordanian timber-processing industries and Saudi pharmaceutical ventures. TAIC has also invested in strategic self-sufficiency projects, such as the Kenana Sugar Complex in Sudan, to see if the Arab world's annual 21 billion import bill can be reduced ("SAMA listings," 1984).

The growth in TAIC's interaction in the Saudi banking environment is a testimonial to the increasing sophistication of the Saudi financial system. TAIC's director general says, "Five years ago, if you tried to market any kind of financial service in Saudi Arabia, you would have had very little response" ("SAMA Listings," p. 103). However, this new appetite for banking services is encouraging new service development, and, as the flow-of-funds approach deems necessary, it will help to change the Arab attitude toward money as a tool for transactions purposes only, leading to a demand for money as an investment. Only in this manner can the financial system become an official conduit for transferable savings, and as such promote the economic development of Saudi Arabia and the other Arab countries.

OBSERVATIONS

Islamic Banking as an Instrument of Foreign Policy?

Many Muslim states are willing to utilize Islamic banking as the vehicle in: promoting Islamic solidarity among Muslim nations; cooperating among Muslims in economic, financial, and scientific facets; and working to shield themselves against non-Muslim financial powerhouses.

Limitations of Interest-Free Banking (IFB)

- There appear to be unresolved problems associated with full integration of IFB into the global system.
- A prolonged decrease of oil revenues will diminish the strength of the IFBs globally. Its relevance to the global economy will remain; nevertheless, the reduction of oil revenues has limited people's ability to save, depriving banks of a much-needed source of capital.

With the exception of Iran—though this is open to discussion as well—in the entire Muslim world, both Arab and non-Arab, the masses and the ruling elites are not moving in the same direction. In an attempt to gain religious legitimacy—in view of the weakness of other sources of legitimacy—the ruling elites have resorted and will continue to resort to symbolic or real measures such as the Islamization of the banking system. The fact is that the elites in many oil-rich Muslim nations are on the defensive and have to explain themselves in Islamic terms.

There is no shortcut solution to this phenomena. As long as the social contract/compact between the ruler and the ruled is not adhered to, the "populist Islamist" will grow in strength. The movement is here to stay and will be a powerful force into the next century. Western financial institutions must position themselves to cope with the (new) Islamization process.

The last decade has shown that substantial numbers of consumers are attracted by what Islamic banks have to offer; the banks, as they have drawn more deposits, have gradually developed management expertise and sophistication to match. Clearly, though, this is an industry that is still being born, and problems persist. The fact that many Islamic banks were established during the boom years of the 1980s and 1990s means that while still new and inexperienced, they faced the declining economic performance of many Middle Eastern countries brought about by dwindling oil revenues, decreased trade, and an unstable political environment. These difficulties have highlighted the urgency that most Islamic bankers now agree is their immediate priority: the establishment of a global Islamic capital market that can bring together the providers and users of capital throughout the world. A global marketplace would significantly increase the scope of profit-sharing investments by Islamic banks and impel them to increase the deposit-taking activities of their established networks or retail branches.

CONCLUSION

As suggested in the opening paragraphs of this chapter, modernization and development may be described as the rationalization of the way life and activities are organized. This concept also applies to the development of financial markets. As both developmental monetary theories postulate, there is a process of rationalization that financial markets must pass through in order to contribute to the development of their respective countries. In order for the rationalization process to commence, two important changes must occur. The first must be a change in the attitude toward money as a tool for transactions purposes only. If the fact that a complementary relationship exists between money and capital is never accepted, money will never be seen as a tool for investment. If this attitude change does not occur, financial intermediaries will be useless as channels for the flow of excess savings into more productive areas. The second change must occur in the financial market itself. Policies must be instituted that will free up the "development channels" and permit them to allocate surplus resources efficiently.

Unfortunately, for most developing nations, this requires a commitment from the government to reduce its intervention in the financial market and rely on market forces to determine the interest rate and the appropriate financial instruments most effective in channeling funds from surplus to deficit sectors. Governments have traditionally diminished interest rates in most LDC countries, and although the evidence suggests that this most often leads to negative real interest rates and repressed financial markets, governments continue to set the rates to protect their financial needs and to prevent private competition against state enterprise. Although the liberalization of financial sectors creates the potential danger of excessive profits in oligopolistic, primitive financial markets—which are not yet efficient in the allocation of resources—these short-run profits attract more competition, and in doing so stimulate the growth of the financial sector. There may be less risk associated with the temporary excesses of financial liberalization than with the efforts by governments to impose their ideas of appropriate interest rates and financial structures.

This is not to imply that governments should completely bow out of the picture. Government investment constitutes the largest part of total investment in most developing countries, and it has not yet been established that private investment would increase enough to maintain appropriate development levels if government reduced its activities. Consequently, there may be a case for government entry into the financial market, possibly in the form of a government bank, as long as its function is to stimulate competition among private firms.

As one can see, government interaction in developing financial markets is part of the sociological limit to the development of those markets, possibly the most forceful deterrent. In Islamic countries, where Islamic law forbids the payment of interest, financial markets are limited by a biopsychological variable. Although some countries, such as Saudi Arabia, have been able to circumvent these laws, the emergence of "Islamic" banks may provide a solution. The impact of logical limits, which represent the criteria used in choosing the path to development, is lessened somewhat by convergence theory. Convergence theory suggests that all financial markets are headed for the same destination regardless of starting points and intermediate routes. In other words, the criteria of logical limits might slow the process, but once a certain level of modernization is reached, the theory predicts increasing similarity between all financial markets.

It has been established that the development of financial markets follow a rational plan. Moore's theory of world modernization and the limits to convergence trace the modernization process and introduce the need for financial systems. This need is reinforced by the insights of the Shaw-McKinnon framework and elaborated upon by the flow-of-funds approach. The main focus of both developmental theories concerns the creation of financial channels and focuses on increasing their efficiency. In conclusion, the development of financial channels is essential to the modernization of a developing economy, and it is hoped that the growing interdependency that has developed among international financial systems in recent years will speed the development of less-developed financial markets.

REFERENCES

Ajami, R., D. Khambata, and M. Kavoossi (1992). "Interest Free Banking." In D. Siddiqui and A. Alkhafaji (Eds.), *The Gulf War: Implications for Business and Media*. Apollo, Pa.: Closson Press.

"Banking Sector Makes Progress toward Maturity" (1984). *Middle East Economic Digest (MEED)*, Special Report on Saudi Arabia, July.

"Citibank to Market Islamic Equity Fund" (1996). *Middle East Economic Digest*, November 29.

Coats, W. L., and D. R. Khatkhate (1984). "Monetary Policy in Less Developed Countries: Main Issues." *Developing Economies*, No. 22.

Esposito, J. (Ed.) (1980). *Islam and Development*. Syracuse, N.Y.: Syracuse University Press.

"Free the Markets and Develop" (1983). *Euromoney*, May.

"Islamic Banking Gains Momentum, Expands Market and Competes with Conventional Banking in Arab States" (1998). *Middle East Executive Reports*, January.

"Islamic Banks and Financial Institutions: A Survey" (1997). *Journal of Muslim and Minority Affairs*, April 1.

"Islamic Funds Aim to Raise $1,500 Million" (1998). *Middle East Economic Digest (MEED)*, July 24.

Khouri, R. L. (1987). "Islamic Banking: Knotting a New Network." *Armaco World*.

Moore, W. E. (1979). *World Development: The Limits to Convergence*. New York: Elsevier.

"SAMA Listings Signals New Era for TAIC" (1984). *Middle East Economic Digest (MEED)*, Special Report on Saudi Arabia, July.

"Western Banks Taking 1st Steps into Islam's 'No Interest' World" (1997). *American Banker* 162:20, January 30, p. 9.

7

Middle East Free Trade Association (MEFTA)?

This chapter examines the notion that there is no simple relationship between integration, economic development, and expanding trade among selected Middle Eastern states. The study suggests that government intervention and heavy-handed involvement in the market serves as a forceful deterrent to the formation of a free trade arrangement among these countries. The chapter concludes that the conditions necessary for the Middle East to transform itself into a free trade association currently do not exist.

INTRODUCTION

Since the end of the Cold War, Middle Eastern leaders, energized by efforts toward piecemeal resolution of the Arab-Israeli conflict, have scrambled to bring greater peace and harmony to the region. However, on economic grounds, integration still remains an aspiration of the people of the region. Experience has indeed produced a certain degree of skepticism as to the validity of some of the objectives and approaches of the past. Middle Eastern economic integration has not been attempted regionwide. However, there have been attempts among groupings of countries in the Gulf subregion of the Middle East and among specific groups of countries—the Maghreb Economic Community, the Arab Common Market (ACM), the Economic Cooperation Organization (ECO), and the Gulf Cooperation Council (GCC), to name but a few. The GCC and the European Union (EU) are gradually moving toward a free trade zone in two to three years. If agreement is reached, all tariffs and import restrictions would be eliminated over eight to ten years for most products. Presently no such agreement exists among the countries in the region.

The Middle East and North Africa region extends from Mauritania in the west to the Persian Gulf in the east. While uniform in certain elements of culture, such as religion and language (with the exception of the Iranians), the region displays considerable economic and political diversity. This study concentrates on the Islamic states, particularly the Gulf area. Israel is not included in the study, due to the fact that the Israeli economy is basically fed through the West; its trade in the region is minimal. The purpose of this study is to analyze systematically and evaluate political, economic, and cultural factors influencing the prospects for integration, trade, and foreign direct investment among the states.

During most of the histories of Middle Eastern societies, their economies have been agrarian and rural. The need for integration has been minimal; therefore, coexistence with other societies was not too difficult, and interactions were kept at a minimum. This changed abruptly in the 1970s. Many Middle Eastern countries had become rich in petroleum, a commodity in high demand in Western nations. Sales of this commodity brought inconceivable quantities of petrodollars into the region. Suddenly, the states were among the world's largest traders. While the desire for economic development in order to modernize society and bring the region closer to other regions in the world was prevalent, this modernization was to take time. In the meantime, trade expanded, and infrastructural needs to accommodate further economic development skyrocketed.

A second event in the late 1970s also brought to the forefront the existence of fertile grounds for conflict and the need for cooperation. With the ascension of the Ayatollah Khomeini as the societal head of Iran, there was a resurgence in traditional Islamic values and Islamic solidarity, albeit on Iranian terms. This created a major conflict. On the one hand there were the need and means for economic cooperation and modernization, while on the other there was a return of old suspicions and distrust among historically adversarial neighbors.

POST–WORLD WAR II RECORD OF
INTEGRATION: THE CONCEPTUAL DILEMMA

Free trade in the modern era began in Great Britain with the repeal of the corn laws in 1846 and the accompanying tariff reductions. The Anglo-French Treaty of 1860 introduced the concept of most-favored-nation status, which enhanced international trade. This practice provided preferential treatment for selected trading partners, which allowed free movement of goods and services.

The literature on economic integration is impressive, including possible approaches to integration, its modalities, the obstacles related to this process, and NAFTA and other regional integration arrangements (Schott, 1988; Suriyamongkol, 1988; Stockel and Banks 1990).

A historical review of integration literature shows that David Mitrany was among the forerunners of integration theorists in the late nineteenth century. However, his functionalism centered on cooperation among trade unions and associations across national boundaries. F. Machlop (1980) states that the term "integration" in economics was first used in industrial organizations to refer to combined firms. The integration of economies of separate states is not found in economic history literature prior to J. Viner (1950). That author introduced the foundation of the theory of customs unions, which represents the core theory of economic/market integration. Following Viner, the works of Balassa, Robson, Machlop, and Richard Cooper were welcome new additions to the field. They each contributed to the literature by evaluating and analyzing the effects of integration on the national, regional, and global economies. In practice, however, official integration arrangements in the Middle East, with a core of Persian Gulf states, including Bahrain, Iran, Iraq, Kuwait, Saudi Arabia, United Arab Emirates (UAE), and some of the more peripheral states of North Africa, remain nonexistent.

The Middle East's history in the post–World War II period is riddled with attempts to integrate. However, the nature and range of economic activities and the pattern of trade, both regional and international, have shifted from extractive industries and agricultural commodities to more downstream manufacturing industries. In this process there has been some value added to the existing trade, moving away from the trade of simple raw materials to processed and manufactured goods.

Empirical studies indicate that nations that have reached the second or third level of W. W. Rostow's economic development stages have a better chance of forging a working integration arrangement (Rostow, 1964). By the mid-1970s many Middle Eastern states were approaching that stage. Stage one includes the traditional subsistence level of economic development. The second stage is reached when an economy is able to produce some of its basic needs and enjoy some manufacturing capabilities (pre-takeoff stage). The third stage involves the takeoff stage, in which an economy is capable of producing much of its own manufacturing needs and can also export some.

In most societies, rules are followed, beliefs are accepted, and authority is obeyed because that is the way life has always been organized. Common beliefs and practices are the building blocks of an integrated society. The rationales of certain beliefs, practices, and sources of legitimate power have traditional roots. Tradition is an especially important factor. At times, leaders of states have even been worshiped as though they were beings of a higher order. This thinking can become a hindrance to the modernization and economic integration of a society.

The desire for an orderly society led members to use fact and logic in choosing behavior that would propel society toward the achievement of various goals. But, as people took charge of their own destiny, they shifted away from the environment and began to adapt the environment to themselves, providing more order in their existence. Environmental adaptation brought about the development of technology needed to order the natural elements. This move toward rationalization is fundamental to the economic modernization process.

As the use of technology in the modernization process made societies more productive and efficient, production increases led to utilization of the economies of scale where trade increased. With the end of serfdom and feudal property systems, labor markets and enlarged capital markets were realized. Commercialization became more complete and complex, which gave rise to integrated market systems. This integration and consequent development of societal economics was and still is a crucial mechanism for the rationalization of exchange and distribution.

MARKET INTEGRATION AND THE DEVELOPING NATIONS OF THE MIDDLE EAST

In subsistence economies, market integration is minimal and often nonexistent. Producers and investors tend to be identical, and most private investment depends on prior accumulation of capital. Trade policies to help protect the owner of capital, and reliance on heavy government expenditure, have been the major components of the economic and trade policies and processes in these countries.

Markets in more sophisticated developing countries are often inefficient and dominated by heavy-handed state-owned enterprises. The primary trade is in raw materials or in processed natural resources. Other products, such as light manufacturing, strive to break through the international or regional markets. There is intense competition with neighboring economies for access to export markets. Since the government plays such a large role in the economies of less developed countries (LDCs), there is usually balanced trade, which is brought about by export/import controls.

If long-term growth and development is the objective, trade policy should be directed toward the eradication of inefficiencies existing in the various sectors of the LDCs. The role of trade must be viewed in developing countries as that of a distribution agent through which the unproductive sectors of the economy are channeled to other sectors where internalization and sector integration takes place. This developmental role of trade can be described by the developmental theories linking trade and economic integration to development.

Such theories stipulate that more rapid growth requires more investment in trade-based industries and manufacturing. The focus of trade and development theories is on increasing the flow of goods and services from the surplus sectors into the integrated markets, and on increasing the level of trade balances. This objective is not simply to increase aggregate trade but to promote transferrable factors of production by increasing the ratio of differentiated investments to total trade.

Empirical evidence indicates that the elasticity of demand for goods and services is related to the stages of economic development. As markets become better organized, the range of products offered is widened. The higher the level of economic development, the more integrated an economy becomes. This allows markets to produce a wide variety of goods and services.

Empirical studies have established that trade among the Persian Gulf states of the Middle East is not unrestricted but that it is fairly protectionist (*Foreign Trade Barriers*, 1993). This evidence indicates that there is no proper channel for the utilization of comparative national or corporate competitive advantages. The absence of coordinated and enforced intellectual property protection serves as a fur-

Table 7.1: Selected Middle East Countries' Trade Barriers				
	Intellectual Property Protection		Standards	Government Procurement	Other
	Copyrights	Patents	Certification	Purchasing Domestic	Export Subsidies
Bahrain	-	*	-	*	-
Iran	-	*	*	-	*
Kuwait	-	-	-	*	*
Oman	-	-	-	*	*
Qatar	-	-	-	*	*
Saudi Arabia	*	*	*	*	*
UAE	-	-	-	*	*

Source: Compiled from *Foreign Trade Barriers*, Washington, D.C., 1993.

ther deterrent. Government procurement, standards, testing, labeling, and export subsidies are common practice.

It seems that markets in the Middle Eastern countries provide goods and services to the public but do little in the way of channeling surplus goods or services into productive sectors, either domestically or across national boundaries. Annually non-oil intraregional exports amount to about 19 percent on the average among the Arab states of the Middle East. Market distortions caused by government intervention and inadequate transportation prevent free flow of goods and services produced. (See Table 7.1.)

ISLAMIC ECONOMICS AND INTEGRATION

The previous discussion points to primary issues of conflict in the development of a free trade association among developing countries, including the Middle East. These issues include:

- Socio-economic differences
- Level of economic development
- Political factors and considerations
- Cultural factors, such as religion and language.

As stated earlier, the basic function of trade is to act as an arbiter of consumption and production in channeling goods and services, as an efficient allocator of factors of production in a free-moving trade environment. This process furthers economic growth and subsequent economic development, which is desperately needed today in most Middle Eastern nations. The challenge is to devise a system that promotes this activity while preserving the current standard of living in the participating nations, as well as Islamic values.

One can reasonably argue that Islamic economics is not much different from the familiar Western economics that prevails the world over. The only difference is that Islamic economics is not based on Adam Smith–style capitalism. From this perspective, the Islamic pattern of trade not only does not lead to inequality among nations but reduces existing inequalities. Therefore, Islamic economists come very close to Western economists on the issue of economic integration, through the eventual leveling effect of economic development.

ECONOMIC FEATURES AND ISSUES OF THE MIDDLE EAST

There has been a general economic stagnation in the Mideast region since the early 1980s. While the region performed fairly well in the 1970s, annual economic growth declined sharply to an average of 0.5 percent per year in the 1980s and did not improve significantly in the 1990s, in spite of its good resource endowment. However, in studying this phenomenon, four additional factors should be taken into account to illustrate some of the distortions at work.

First, about one-half of the region's food comes from outside the region, with little interregional agricultural trade, given the similarity of crop production. The only two countries capable to some degree of food and agricultural export, Iran and Iraq, have remained inactive or incapacitated for various reasons:

- An eight year Iran-Iraq war, which diverted national resources away from agriculture.
- The 1991 Gulf war and the subsequent United Nations economic and trade sanctions on Iraq.

Secondly, the region's industrial base remains extractive. For the region as a whole, it is estimated that extractive industries generate more than two-thirds of the value-added in the economy, which is dominated by petroleum and natural gas. Generally, industrial development in the region indicates some progress. Nevertheless, the role of manufacturing in the regional economy remains limited in comparison with other developing countries, such as India, Turkey, Indonesia, Malaysia, Singapore, or China. The pattern of international trade reveals a high degree of dependency on OECD countries, in particular in the areas of transfer of technology or sources of capital. It is estimated that less than 6 percent of the region's exports to the OECD represents manufactured goods. The larger portion of the region's imports are manufactured products developed in industrialized countries. The region relies heavily on foreign patents, technical know-how, engineering designs, and management.

Another factor to consider is that with a few exceptions, the countries in the region may be facing a water crisis in the not-distant future. Most water supplies are cross-national, leading to increased tension and possible conflict, giving greater urgency for cooperation on this front. This is important, because if water resources are not adequately shared, a process of economic protectionism and a trend toward disintegration could result.

Finally, on the issue of economic management, the largest economies in the region suffer from chronic economic problems. Iran is faced with unemployment, high inflation, and a high debt burden, aggravated by U.S.-imposed sanctions in 1995. Iraq, faced with United Nations sanctions, suffers from the most fundamental economic problems and a deteriorating infrastructure. Saudi Arabia suffers from high trade and budget deficits, and a widening income disparity. Bahrain, Kuwait, the United Arab Emirates, and Qatar have successfully stabilized their economies in the aftermath of the Gulf war and declining oil revenues, while facing increased military expenditures, and have resumed a path toward stable economic growth. However, others, such as Oman and Yemen, are still confronted with enormous challenges and systems of governments that lack responsiveness, accountability, and predictability. Perhaps with the exception of Iran, this is true for most of the nations discussed above. (See Table 7.2.)

In addition, the following elements serve as forceful limits to an effective integration arrangement:

- Legal and political uncertainties
- Slowdown of privatization process in some of the key countries, including Iran
- Underdeveloped financial markets.

Table 7.2: Direction of Trade: The Three Largest Economies in the Gulf, 1993, 1995 (billions of U.S.$)				
	Imports		Exports	
	1993	1995	1993	1995
Iran	16.0	14.0	12.0	12.9
Saudi Arabia	30.0	28.0	22.0	46.0
UAE	20.0	21.0	24.5	26.0

Sources: Direction of Trade Statistics Yearbook, International Monetary Fund, 1994 and *World Development Report 1997*, Washington, D.C.: World Bank; *Middle East Economic Digest* (September 25, 1998).

Nevertheless, some basic elements for economic integration seem to exist and are potentially promising:

• The region is relatively rich in resources; two-thirds of the total known oil and gas reserves are located in the region.
• The proximity of the region to Europe, Africa, and the markets of the newly independent states (NIS), as well as to Indonesia, Thailand, Malaysia, and Singapore, is of strategic significance in the new international economic order.
• The region has a diversified, relatively large, skilled, and inexpensive labor force.
• An entrepreneurial tradition exists that is absent in many other parts of the world, as well as a historical experience with initiative and an orientation to private enterprise.

MOTIVES FOR MEFTA (MIDDLE EAST FREE TRADE ASSOCIATION)

Closer trade links between Middle Eastern countries will generate gains for the member states. First, there will be specialization and efficiency gains from the exploitation of the traditional comparative advantages of trading partners, gains from the availability of a greater variety of goods, and possibly, efficiency gains from economies of scale and increased competition. Second, first-round gains in efficiency and output will provide a second-round boost to output over the medium term. Increased efficiency in the first round will raise the return to capital, thereby leading to increased investment. Saving will also rise, either because of higher returns to savings or because part of the initial increase in output is saved, or both. In an empirical study (Levin and Renalt, 1992), researchers provide evidence that increased openness leads to higher levels of investment. The second-round effect could take the form of permanent increases in the rate of output if there are sufficient spillovers or economies of scale.

In theory, such growth could happen in several ways. For example, trade integration could allow firms to spread the cost of research and development over a larger market, thus reducing unit costs and encouraging greater innovation and technical progress. This can, in turn, generate positive spillovers as successful innovations are applied more broadly. Furthermore, integration can also boost productivity growth, allowing increased specialization. In this regard, MEFTA is not going to be any different than other integration arrangements, such as NAFTA.

Estimating the actual gains from growing trade integration is very difficult; however, MEFTA would need to implement the following recommendations, to start with.

• Abolition of all quantitative import restrictions
• Phasing out of all tariffs on imports of industrial goods from member states
• Extended preferential access for agriculture exports to member states.

Several other motives can be advanced toward the creation of MEFTA. Generally, economic integration is advocated for political reasons. It tends to reduce conflict, providing a common ground for shared interests, thereby enabling countries to direct resources to economic development. Economic factors, however, are equally important. Cooperation in trade enlarges markets and improves terms of trade of the regional trade blocs in relation to the rest of the world, by increasing leverage and possibly their bargaining power. It allows for the emergence of efficient manufacturing and the possible recognition of the comparative advantages of nations. Economic integration increases production arising from specialization. It induces changes affecting factor inputs; capital flows can improve the allocation of resources between countries. Many infrastructural and environmental projects can be implemented only in a regional context; such projects hold the promise of contributing both to economic prosperity and lasting peace. By clarifying the parameters of an eventual MEFTA, trade may increase the welfare of the integrated groups by utilizing the economies of scale, free flow of goods and services, capital flow, and subsequent increases in jobs and income.

MEFTA: PROSPECTS AND LIMITATIONS

While much of the world is moving toward economic blocs; the Middle East seems to have fallen behind this trend. This may be attributed to several socio-economic factors hindering the process, not unlike those found in other regional groupings:

1. Inadequate willingness on the part of the political leadership in many countries to move beyond parochialism to regionalism, resisting possible diminution of national sovereignty.
2. Uneven levels of economic development as well as significant differences in the economic systems of potential participants.
3. Uneven market sizes and the sizes of GNPs, which causes smaller states to fear domination by their bigger neighbors.
4. Absence of grassroots consumer groups and business interest groups to advance and embark on a national debate on the issues relating to integration. In general, this refers to the inadequacies and unrepresentative nature of many Middle Eastern states.
5. No clear engine of economic growth or powerhouse in the region that can serve as a possible "Germany of the Middle East" to pull along others, at least in the initial stages.
6. Absence of strong, independent judiciary for speedy conflict resolution.

However, prospects for a potential MEFTA remain promising. While past records are not very encouraging and many hurdles remain in place, an empirical study demonstrates that the advantages of integration can be significant for the region (J. E. Zarouk, 1992). This study indicates that a 100 percent removal of tariff barriers among the Arab Middle Eastern nations will increase intraregional trade by about $1.5 billion at the end of the first five years of the implementation, and by 5.2 billion at the end of ten years.

CONCLUSION

As suggested here, modernization and development may be described as rationalization of the way life and activities are organized. This concept also applies to the development of integrated markets.

As market integration theory postulates, there is a process of rationalization that markets must pass through in order to develop their respective economies. In order for the rationalization process to commence, two important changes must occur. The first must be a change in attitude toward integration as a means for furthering economic development and modernization. If the complementary relationship that exists between integration and development is not accepted, trade will not be seen as a tool for development. If this attitude change does not occur, market intermediaries, such as free trade associations, will be useless as channels for attaining comparative advantage and economies of scale. The second change must occur in the marketplace itself. Policies must be instituted that will free up trade by developing intraregional channels and permit them to allocate surplus resources efficiently.

Unfortunately for most developing nations, including the Middle East, this requires a commitment from government to reduce its intervention in the market and rely on market forces to determine supply and demand and the prices most effective in channeling funds and resources from surplus areas to deficit sectors. Governments have traditionally administered markets in most Middle Eastern countries, and although the evidence suggests that this has most often led to negative performance and repressed markets, governments continue to set strict boundaries for free enterprise, to protect their own political interests and to prevent private-sector competition against state enterprises. Although the liberalization of markets creates the potential danger of excessive profits in oligopolistic, monopolistic markets—which are not efficient in the allocation of resources—these short-run profits will attract more competition and in doing so stimulate the growth of markets. There may be less risk associated with the temporary excesses of trade liberalization than in efforts by governments to improve their ideas of appropriate market behavior and market structures.

This is not to imply that government should completely bow out of the picture. Government investment contributes the largest part of the total investment in most Middle Eastern countries, and it has not yet been established that private investment would increase enough to maintain appropriate development levels if government reduced its activities. Consequently, there may be a case for government entry into the market, possibly in the form of government guarantees, financial as well as technical assistance, and provision of working capital to importers and exporters, as long as its function is to stimulate competition among private firms. Government interaction in the Middle East is part of the sociological limit to development of these markets, and it might well be the most forceful deterrent.

The conditions necessary for the Middle East to transform itself into a free trade association currently do not exist. Middle Eastern countries have succeeded only in providing a framework within which a number of states have transformed and corrected their relations with one another, based on bilateral or multilateral arrangements. As global competition increases and countries within trading blocs gain added advantage, Middle Eastern countries need to forge closer ties to remain viable and relevant in the twenty-first century.

REFERENCES

Alkhafaji, A. (1992). *The Gulf War: Implications for Global Business and Media*. Apollo, Pa.: Closson Press.

Balaassa, B. (1961). *The Theory of Economic Integration*. Homewood, Ill.: Richard D. Irwin.

Cooper, R. (1987). *Economic Policy in an Interdependent World*. Cambridge, Mass.: MIT Press.

Foreign Trade Barriers (1993). U.S. Government publication, Washington D.C.: Office of the United States Trade Representative.

International Monetary Fund (1994). *Direction of Trade Statistics Yearbook*. Washington, D.C.

Levin, R., and D. Renalt (1992). "A Sensitivity Analysis of Cross-Country Growth Regression." *American Economic Review* 82, 942–963.

Machlop, F. (1980). *Economic Integration: Worldwide, Regional, Sectoral*. London: Macmillan.

Maurice, S., and A. L. Winters (May 1998). "Dynamics and Politics in Regional Integration Arrangements: An Introduction." *World Bank Economic Review* 12:2.

Moore, W. (1979). *World Development: Limits to Convergence*. New York: Elsevier.

Rostow, W. W. (1964). *The Stages of Economic Growth*. Cambridge: Cambridge University Press.

Schott, J. (1988). *United States–Canada Free Trade: An Evaluation of the Agreement*. Washington, D.C.: Institute for International Economics.

Stockel, A., and G. Banks (1990). *Western Trade Blocs*. Canberra, Australia: Center for International Economics.

Suriyamongkol, M. (1988). *Politics of Asian Economic Cooperation*. Oxford: Oxford University Press.

Viner, J. (1950). *The Customs Union Issue*. New York: Carnegie Endowment for International Peace.

Zarrouk, J. E. (1992). "Intra-Arab Trade: Determinants and Prospects for Expansion." In El Najar Said (Ed.), *Foreign and Intra-Trade Politics of the Arab Countries*. Washington, D.C: IMF.

8

The Economic Cooperation Organization (ECO): Opening Doors to Cooperation?

This chapter is directed toward a better understanding of how some of the Islamic countries that are members of the Economic Cooperation Organization (ECO) are impacting the economic and business potential of the organization. Three major nations have been selected for analysis: Azerbaijan, Iran, and Turkey. The policies of these countries will be analyzed to identify the real and potential impacts that such policies have on this regional cooperation organization as well as on the domestic economies of the nations in question. The study further discusses the strategic positioning or intent of these nations and whether they are conducive to greater cooperation or lead to potential conflict.

LITERATURE REVIEW

The increasing importance of economic integration research as a means of understanding the complexities of business environment and factors influencing competitiveness has been gaining strength in recent years (Pomfret, 1997; Mark, 1997; Temple, 1994). Empirical research dealing with integration among the ECO members remains the exception rather than the rule. Banuazizi and Weiner (1994) and Tarock and Sewy (1997), among others, understood the lack of systematic research dealing with the impact of integration on the economies of the member states of ECO.

A review of the scarce empirical-based literature related to the impact of economic integration on selected member countries is in order.

Government-inspired restrictions on trade of goods, services, and factors of production across national boundaries operate asymmetrically. Moreover, these policies are indigenous to the nature of economic integration. Exposure to foreign trade is strongly and positively correlated with the size of government (as a share of GDP). Governments in the more open economies tend to be bigger. They consume, transfer, and invest higher shares of national income. Swietochoski analyzes the triangular relationship between Azerbaijan, Iran, and Turkey. He traces the historical roots of cooperation and sources of conflict among the countries to the present date.

OBJECTIVES OF THE CHAPTER

This chapter will attempt to identify the strategic dimensions in which the countries under study are competing along—or are possibly positioning themselves, or being positioned by—external forces. It further attempts to analyze whether these dimensions could converge and serve the interest of the strategic group through cooperation, or diverge, leading to a fragmented structure with an increased degree of rivalry. This will partly depend on the willingness of the respective governments to cooperate rather than compete for influence in the region. The success or failure of this cooperation will determine whether there will be an engine of economic growth for ECO.

Two of the three original members, Iran and Turkey, have undertaken substantial liberalization measures in recent years, while Azerbaijan has dismantled the mechanism of central planning and seems to be committed to the creation of a market-based economy.

The chapter will also note the following observations:

- The three selected states are not involved in any military conflict.
- Iran and Turkey seem to be competing for influence in Azerbaijan.
- The economy of Azerbaijan seems to be still integrated into the former Soviet Union (FSU). The process of disengagement needs to be further analyzed. Is this entanglement a threat or a complement to ECO?

- The three selected states enjoy a significant degree of Azeri and Islamic heritage.

Motivated by practical and theoretical issues raised here, the significance of this line of research leads to the formulation of the following research hypotheses:

- Integration in the context of strategic intent and interests of the members to enhance their competitiveness vis-à-vis each other and the outside world; compatibility of competitive strategy of nations and integration.
- Openness of economy (factor mobility) and government involvement in the economy among the countries under study.

Each of the hypotheses focus on a specific aspect of the project; combined, they address both the managerial and leadership factors related to integration in ECO.

POTENTIAL CONTRIBUTION OF THE STUDY

With the exception of ASEAN in Asia, and perhaps the recently formed MERCOSUR in South America, the history of integration among developing countries is not promising. This study will attempt to expand discussion and understanding in a newly emergent developing area of the world—the Caspian Sea region, with a vast reservoir of critical and strategic natural resources. It will further test the validity of economic openness and of government involvement in the economy in an area of the world previously not included in studies.

A NEED FOR STRATEGY

Distortion of economic development and unequal distribution of national infrastructure characterizes the main economic commonality among the ten ECO member states. The former Soviet Union (FSU) states, such as Azerbaijan (a heavily subsidized economy), Turkey (a free-market, Westward-oriented society), and Iran (an Islamic-centered state) constitute three of the key players in the critical, strategic region of the Caspian Sea.

ECO, the successor to the now-defunct Regional Cooperation for Development (RCD) Treaty of Izmir, signed by Iran, Pakistan, and Turkey, is now under great pressure to perform. It held its fifth summit on May 11, 1998, in Almaty, Kazakhstan.

The Economic Cooperation Organization was founded in 1985 by Iran, Pakistan, and Turkey to promote economic, technical, and cultural cooperation among the member states. In 1992, some new members—Afghanistan, Azerbaijan, Kazakhstan, Kyrgyzstan, Tajikistan, Turkmenistan, and Uzbekistan—joined ECO.

Against this background of development, however, fundamental issues, in part due to the influence of the organization's more powerful neighbors, remain unresolved. This study will focus on Azerbaijan, Iran, and Turkey as the three most strategically situated of the member states. Azerbaijan and Iran are critically short of capital, and foreign investors are still shying away from all but a few opportunities. Both countries are under U.S. trade sanctions. Turkey is aggressively protecting its secular identity, particularly in an attempt to secure access to the more lucrative Western markets. The major oil producer, Iran in particular, has few profitable operations to discuss with Turkey and Azerbaijan, but they all seem to be preoccupied in positioning themselves in the competitive configuration of the region's structure so as best to defend their interests against competing forces. However, Azerbaijan is yet to articulate its national economic interests concretely and set in motion policies that can lead to the achievement of those interests, even though it enjoys a significant geo-economic advantage.

The three states—Turkey, a major gas market; Azerbaijan, an oil producer, and Iran, a major oil and gas producer and a potential transit country—can be expected to exert increasing influence in the region. Both Iran and Azerbaijan are eager to be future suppliers to Turkey, as evidenced by long-term energy agreements between Turkey and Iran. Meanwhile, Iran, encouraged by Azerbaijan, is making headway in becoming incorporated into petroleum projects in the Caspian region. Washington has decided not to protest the Turkmenistan-Turkey pipeline through Iran.

PROSPECTS FOR REGIONAL INTEGRATION WITHIN ECO

One of the characteristics of the three ECO members is the poorly developed transport network among them. They all have access to waterways, but their road and rail networks were constructed with inward orientations, toward the center, usually the major domestic population centers. While Azerbaijan's network is directed toward Russia, Iran's and Turkey's are directed away from the former USSR. An essential step toward promoting intra-ECO trade is to improve the transit links, and this requires coordination, for which ECO could provide the setting. In the recent summit's Almaty Declaration, the participants agreed upon future cooperation among the member states in the areas of transportation. Details remain to be worked out.

The 1992 enlargement of ECO provided an opportunity to change trade partners. This began to happen immediately after Azerbaijan gained independence, and trade expanded especially between that newly independent state (NIS) and Iran and Turkey. This trade was primarily conducted by individual merchants seeking consumer goods and quick profits previously unavailable in Azerbaijan. The ECO members Iran and Turkey are not leading global suppliers of consumer goods, and they may have difficulty in competing with the newly industrialized countries (NICs) of Asia, especially China or India, as the latter may seek new export markets in the aftermath of their nuclear testing, with the ensuing U.S. economic sanctions and the European Union's negative reactions.

A BRIEF HISTORICAL OVERVIEW

If Samuel Huntington turns out to be accurate in his assertion of cultural determinism (Huntington, 1997) then Iran, Azerbaijan, and Turkey may already be on the right side of history. Given certain strong commonalities among many elements of their culture, it would be safe to predict that they will contribute greatly in terms of enhanced trade and economic cooperation among themselves.

However, it has not always been so in the recent history of these three neighboring countries, particularly in the twentieth century. The Soviet Union denied Azerbaijan the opportunity to experience the "normal" process of becoming an independent nation-state. The coerced inclusion of Azerbaijan into the Soviet Union delayed the socioeconomic development that would have allowed the country to determine its competitive advantages.

In addition, Soviet rule over Azerbaijan was the most serious challenge and threat to a set of religious and ethnic identities deeply rooted in the history of the region (Tarock, 1997). The Soviet period was an era in which the very fabric of Azerbaijani culture was controlled, manipulated, repressed, and eradicated through language reform, resettlement of a Russian population there, educational reforms, and elimination of Islamic institutions and the Muslim clerical class. Muslim Azerbaijanis were confronted with alien political ideologies, cultural traditions, and technologies. It is interesting to note that at about the time of the Bolshevik revolution, both Iran and Turkey were undergoing similar secularization processes, if neither so severe nor by foreign forces. Under Kemal Ataturk in Turkey and Reza Shah Pahlavi in Iran, who both had anticlerical tendencies, this process of "modernization" as well as secularization eroded the culture from Islamic tendencies, including the language in the case of Turkey. This process continued under the reign of Mohammad Reza Shah.

As with the Bolshevik revolution, the Young Turk movement, and the Reza Shah coup, the sudden disintegration of the Soviet system (and a few years earlier the Iranian revolution) allowed little time for the people of Azerbaijan and Iran or Turkey to achieve a gradual establishment of new civil institutions. In other words, the process was rapid, unplanned, unbalanced, and haphazard.

The emergence of a newly independent Azerbaijan, which historically has been in Iran's and Turkey's spheres of political and cultural influence (Tarock, 1997), initially seemed too convenient a field of competition for the two rivals to ignore. However, evidence points to cooperation as well. In fact, the priority of Iran and Turkey (two of the founders of the ECO) has been to incorporate Azerbaijan into ECO. At a summit meeting in Tehran in 1992, Iran played an important role in bringing Azerbaijan into that organization.

However, for these countries to implement ambitious developmental programs, such as road transport, courts, and communications, requires massive foreign investment or assistance from international financial institutions, such as the World Bank and its associates. This process has been burdened by U.S. sanctions against Iran and Azerbaijan and its influence over international financial entities. (See Table 8.1.)

OTHER INTERREGIONAL TENDENCIES

It is important to note that while Turkey has enjoyed preferential trade relations with the European Union (EU), Iran is not a member

Table 8.1: Key Economic Indicators (U.S. $ million) Azerbaijan				
	1993	1994	1995	1996
GDP Growth (%)	-23	-22	-17	-5
GDP (per capita)	443	360	321	297
Govt. Expend. (% of GDP)	NA	46	27	28
Inflation	1,130	1,664	85	28
Unemployment	NA	NA	17	20
Debt Service Ratio	10	10	10	10

Note: All figures are unofficial estimates.

Sources: International Trade Administration (ITA), "Country Commercial Guides," 2/1998; *Trade within and outside ECO and World Development Report*, Washington, D.C.: World Bank, 1999.

of any other regional integration arrangement. It has recently applied for membership in the World Trade Organization (WTO). It is equally important to notice two other integration arrangements established in the post-Soviet era that could stimulate a greater degree of cooperation among the ECO members.

The first Commonwealth of Independent States (CIS) customs union was established between Kazakhstan, Kyrgyzstan, and Uzebekistan in 1994. In March 1996, Russia, Belarus, Kazakhstan, and Kyrgyzstan committed themselves to a single market, which envisages the free movement of goods, services, labor, and capital among the signatories. It is equally important to note that they opted to remain under a ruble zone, in terms of currency arrangements. That meant that they would use the ruble as a medium of exchange, to be accepted by all members. In the same year, 1996, Russia and Belarus founded a commonwealth of sovereign republics, calling for complete economic integration, with a common currency and coordination of foreign and defense policies (Kaser, 1997).

The exploitation of oil is the obvious primary economic direction amongst the three: oil in Azerbaijan and Iran, gold and copper in Iran, copper in Turkey, and bauxite in Azerbaijan. Great expectations are placed on natural gas and on joint ventures with world oil and gas companies. In Azerbaijan, agriculture could become a substantial export earner. Export prospects among manufacturers are far weaker, but low labor costs should offer a competitive advantage. (See Table 8.2.)

Table 8.2: Key Economic Indicators (U.S. $ million) Turkey			
	1994	1995	1996
GDP Growth (%)	-5	7	7
GDP (per capita)	2,151	2,755	2,872
Govt. Expend. (% of GDP)	12	14	15
Inflation	75	80	85
Unemployment Rate (%)	9	7	6
Debt Service Ratio (%)	7	6	5

Sources: U.S. Department of State, "Economic Policy and Trade Practices," Washington, D.C., July 1997; *World Development Report*, Washington, D.C.: World Bank, 1999.

In principle, trade among the three ECO states would be promoted by facilitating payments in hard currency and by the reduction of tariffs. These ideas are under consideration, but progress is very slow.

THE RUSSIAN FACTOR

Moscow's long-term strategies concerning relationships between Azerbaijan, Iran, and Turkey have been supplemented by anxieties over oil. Moscow faces the birth of a world-class petroleum complex in the Caspian Sea region, whether Russia is a part of it or not, and it is determined to hamper any such evolution unless Russia has a say in its future shape. In this they are joined by Iran. Moscow at first exercised blatant political muscle to try to halt the export of Azerbaijani oil via any route that bypasses Russia—especially by a pipeline through Iran and Turkey, but the Chechnya conflict diminished the utility and security of its own routes (Mark, 1997).

Russia has placed further pressure on Baku by restricting the traffic of goods between it and Azerbaijan, on the pretext of Russian security needs arising from the Chechnya conflict (Mark, 1997).

Azerbaijan's economy is weak and will remain so until the flow of oil in the international markets is significantly increased. Of the available resources, much is utilized by the military. There has been little structural reform or private-enterprise initiative. Basic needs are largely met through European Union (EU), Iranian, and Turkish assistance. Even though Azerbaijan is a member of the CIS, there is little in the way of assistance from the member states. Russia, with a GNP exceeding $400 billion in 1996 and a per capita income of over

$2,240, dominates the political and economic affairs of the CIS. Russia generates two-thirds of the economic activity of the member states.

THE U.S. FACTOR

The mounting financial stakes in the Caspian Sea for Western (mainly U.S.) petroleum companies has created a powerful force driving toward Baku.

The development and exploration deals that Azerbaijan has signed with major U.S. oil companies may be added to a series of such arrangements dating back to September 24, 1994, and the signing of the $7.5 billion "contract of the century" between the Azerbaijan International Operating Company (AIOC)—a consortium of Western petroleum companies—and SOCAR, Azerbaijan's state oil company (MEI, November/December 1997). By June 1997, total Western investment in Azerbaijan had reached $18 billion. Some Azerbaijani authorities have asserted that the United States alone has invested $25 billion in the economy (Pomfret, 1997).

The military cooperation agreement Azerbaijan and the United States signed in July 1997 may be viewed as a continuation of U.S.-Azerbaijan cooperation in security and strategic areas. It appears to be a shift toward the West, perhaps to position the country so as to offset Russian, Iranian, and perhaps Turkish pressure.

THE TURKISH FACTOR

For Turkey, Azerbaijan provides both opportunity and risk: opportunity in that it may become a pipeline link and trade route between Azerbaijan and the Mediterranean, and serve as a secular model for the Azerbaijanis; risk, because at a time of foreign policy disappointments with the West (EU rejection of its membership application) and its rejection by the Muslim countries because of its close military association with Israel, Turkey may seek inroads into the affairs of Azerbaijan as a convenient relief from its perceived isolation. Such moves, however, would be perceived as threatening by the Tajiks, Iranians, Afghans, and even the Chinese, not to speak of the Russians.

President Turgut Ozal's economic policy can be safely characterized as export driven. He has put in place a great many export incentives, which partially contributed to corruption, by which some firms have taken advantage of government assistance. This drive, however, originally did not include other ECO members. Nevertheless, this push toward exports is partially to blame for exacerbating the gap between the haves and have nots in Turkey. This explains to some extent the rise of the Islamists, led by Prime Minister Necmettin Erbakan, into power. The dilemma that faces Turkey, as relates to its foreign economic and trade relations, is how to open the economy further without losing control; this is a common problem among the three ECO member states.

Among the ECO members under discussion, possibly after Azerbaijan itself, Turkey is the single biggest beneficiary of the collapse of the Soviet Union. Along with its greater foreign policy flexibility in the region, Turkey has witnessed in recent years a greater degree of popular input into foreign policy formulation. Minorities have increased their roles in the shaping and direction of foreign policy. This gradual "democratization" of foreign policy has provided the Turkish government with greater impetus to engage the newly independent states (NIS), specifically Azerbaijan.

Turkish foreign policy has been equally influenced by emerging tensions between the Islamists, symbolized by Erbekan, and the nationalists, represented by the military and forces aligned with it.

Some of the key foreign policy issues of Turkey at the moment can be prioritized as:

- The Balkans, specifically Bosnia
- The Greek-Cyprus issue
- Russia and the remarkably high degree of economic interaction, particularly Turkish involvement in the construction industry
- The Albanian and Macedonian situation, as it relates to the Turks
- The Caucasus, especially Azerbaijan, Armenia, Georgia, and the Ukraine
- Iran, particularly the Islamist movement's appeal and Iran's foreign policy ambitions in the region
- The EU, particularly in the aftermath of its rejection of Turkey's bid for membership
- The United States, with added significance as the only major Western partner at the time
- Central Asia, essentially in a geo-economic setting. No clear, sustained foreign policy direction has emerged with regard to this region yet.

As for Azerbaijan, despite their initial enthusiasm in approaching the new republic, neither Turkey nor Iran possesses the necessary economic, industrial, or financial resources to exercise a dominant influence over the country. Neither the Islamist orientation of the Iranians nor the secular pan-Turkism of the Turks seems to have much appeal among a dominant majority of Azerbaijanis (Banuazizi and Weiner, *The Geopolitics of Central Asia and Borderlands*).

What seems to be emerging, however, is a genuine desire on the part of the countries for a greater degree of regional cooperation, including in the Economic Cooperation Organization (ECO). For any regional economic cooperation to produce reasonably positive results, there must emerge a dominant organizing principle across national boundaries that utilizes commonalities and exploits the inequalities in the distribution of the national infrastructures of each country.

THE IRAN FACTOR

The emergence of Azerbaijan as a new independent neighbor of Iran has brought new challenges as well as economic and trade opportunities. In establishing close political and trade relations with Azerbaijan, Iran is faced with a number of strong competitors, including Turkey, Russia, China and the United States, which has traditionally attempted to sabotage any Iranian inroad into the newly independent states, especially Azerbaijan, due to its oil interests. Despite such attempts and other competitors, Iran has nevertheless made some notable achievements in the region (Tarock & Sewy, 1997). Right from the start, Iran managed its relations with the new republic from the position of an already existing friendship and goodwill. On the political level, Iran has been careful to avoid giving credibility to the fears expressed in the West and in Russia that it might be tempted to push Azerbaijan toward radical Islam. On the economic level, Iran's activity and success has been modest. (See Table 8.3.) This is partly because its own economy has been weak and, therefore, unable to invest much in the developmental projects in the republic or enter into joint ventures with other countries in order to do so. It is also because private companies and businesspeople in Iran have had little experience investing in foreign countries. In addition, the economic sanctions against Iran imposed by the United States have further handicapped the ability of Iranian businesses to compete or cooperate

Table 8.3: Key Economic Indicators (U.S. $ millions) Iran			
	1994	1995	1996
GDP Growth (%)	5	4	3
GDP (per capita)	NA	NA	1,900
GDP Govt. Expend. (%)	NA	20	20
Inflation	15	15	20
Unemployment	20	20	12
Debt Service Ratio	7	6	5

Sources: World Development Report (WDR), 1995 and 1999, World Bank, Oxford University Press; D. Pearl (1998), "Rial Problems: Economic Woes Complicate Any Thaw with the U.S.," *Wall Street Journal*, June 19.

with their Turkish counterparts in Azerbaijan. In addition, the negative "country of origin" connected with Iran reduces the enthusiasm of Azeri businesses to represent or engage in Iranian business activities.

Iran's relations with Azerbaijan cannot be divorced from its relations with Armenia, Russia, Turkey, and Turkemenistan. Iran's interest in the republic has several dimensions: national security, economics and trade, as well as cultural. For the first time in over 120 years, Iran feels relatively secure in its northern borders. It appears that it has attempted to enhance its degree of cooperation with the NISs in order to ease its strategic encirclement, which extends from Afghanistan to Iraq and the Gulf states. In addition, the relative bewilderment of the United States and its modest influence in the region provides Iran with an opportune time to counterbalance its strategic alliances with the Arab states in the south. At the moment, the Iranians find themselves isolated from the influential Muslim states of Saudi Arabia and Egypt; given Iran's strategic intentions in the region, they find this position unacceptable. Progress having been slow in normalization of relations with these countries, ECO gains a greater sense of urgency.

Iran's overtures to Azerbaijan are motivated not only by security considerations or regional competition with Turkey. Iran sees itself as a trade partner in the areas of gas, oil, and food items. In early 1992, the minister of oil visited Baku to explore the possibility of using Azeri territory for the export of oil to the European markets, and also of using Azeri refineries for Iranian crude.

FACTOR CONDITIONS CONSIDERED FOR ECO
(SELECTED MEMBERS)

- The growth of trade relative to GDP growth rates of the three member countries has been much higher than prior to the formation of ECO. This includes the recessionary period of 1991–1993, when average GDP growth was very low (*WDR*, 1997).
- Certain factors can work in favor of trade growth among ECO members: desynchronization of business cycles in Azerbaijan, Iran, and Turkey; continuation and even acceleration of growth among the countries; and an effective transfer of funds, through active attraction of private capital to these countries.
- The liberalization moves taken by ECO since the mid 1990s have paved the way for these economies to integrate through trade gains. However, the path toward this process has not been smooth for any member.
- The first phase of trade policy reform in ECO, by which obstacles to exports were reduced, typically involved devaluating exchange rates and reducing quantitative restrictions on imports of intermediate and capital goods. In the second phase, tariffs began to be somewhat reduced. Azerbaijan, Iran, and Turkey initiated reforms, but only Iran and Turkey sustained and even enlarged the level of liberalization. Azerbaijan succeeded in increasing both exports and imports during the adjustment process. However, import growth overtook export growth, due to the growth of the domestic consumer market, which has resulted in persistent balance-of-payment problems.
- Furthermore, liberalization has reduced both import and export impediments. Reforms in Iran and Turkey, the early reformers, were initially characterized by efforts to adjust their currencies. Azerbaijan, the late reformer, had a higher degree of anti-export bias, as well as distortions produced by higher black market activities before the reform. Initially, the black market activities were reduced in these economies, except in Azerbaijan, where higher inflation undermined reform efforts. All three member countries achieved a higher pace of trade integration and market openness. However, unbalanced import-dominant integration is particularly visible in Azerbaijan. Dominance of import growth is also evident for Iran.
- In Azerbaijan, however, the components of trade shifted drastically during the integrated reform, with import growth overtaking export growth as a force in overall trade integration.
- In Turkey, the trade/GDP ratio almost tripled in 1995, as opposed to 17

percent earlier in 1980 (*WDR*, 1997). Although Turkey's export success is still limited in scope, that success has been due to the openness of its import regime and significant real depreciation of the currency, as well as its harmonization of trade policies with the European Union Customs Union. Turkey's commitment to stability in the exchange rate in order to preserve the competitiveness of the export sector can be noted. (*Exchange Rate Arrangements and Restrictions*, IMF 1997). Although, unlike Azerbaijan and Iran, large capital flows had caused pressure on the Turkish lira to appreciate, the government stemmed short-run inflows to avoid revaluation. However, despite these reform measures, Turkey's export growth decelerated from 17 percent a year on average in the 1980s prior to 1990s to 9.5 percent for 1990–95, partly due to the slowdown in the European Union's market (Exchange Rate Arrangements and Restrictions, IMF, 1997).

- Although ECO members are projected to contribute around 12 percent to incremental world trade during the coming decade, prospects for trade integration differ by country. Lagging integration in the Middle East has been and will continue to be dependent on favorable terms of trade and capital flows, for their nations' integration into each other's economy to prosper.

- The largely unilateral trade liberalization among the three ECO member states observed since 1990 represents an effective shift in development strategy from an inward (import-substitution) to an outward-oriented (export-promoting) framework designed to create a cycle of higher integration and factor growth under an expanded opportunity set.

- Another potential problem faced by the three ECO members is that excessive dependence on capital flow puts pressure on currency. Therefore, careful management is called for.

- Balanced integration in ECO calls for sound growth of exports or a firm commitment to future export growth. This can be attained only by a combination of domestic and trade policies that encourage long-term productive investment in the exportable sector.

CONCLUDING OBSERVATIONS

Azerbaijan, Iran, and Turkey have taken the opportunity to expand their links with each other by means of ECO. There exists a healthy degree of rivalry between Iran and Turkey to establish a sphere of economic influence over Azerbaijan.

More importantly, Iran and Turkey are attempting to increase their interdependence among the republics through a massive road and rail network. This will go a long way toward bridging Azerbaijan and Iran's relative political and economic isolation.

Even though the three have substantial cultural ties with each other, they each wish to exploit them with great caution, fearing the unleashing of uncontrollable ethnic emotions. ECO is being presented as a test case for the three states' good intentions. It can help Turkey find a more "natural" economic integration arrangement, one in which it would be a full, founding partner. Furthermore, Azerbaijan can use the bloc to offset excessive reliance on the Russians or the United States. Also, Iran can play a stabilizing, constructive role through the exercise of a nonideological foreign policy, diminishing the fears of its southern neighbors and their Western patrons.

REFERENCES

Banuazizi, A., and M. Weiner (Eds.), (1994). *The New Geopolitics of Central Asia and Its Borderlands*. Bloomington and Indianapolis: Indiana University Press.

Business America (1998). U.S. Department of Commerce. Washington, D.C.: International Trade Administration, February 10.

Country Reports on Economic Policy and Trade Practices (1998). Washington, D.C.: U.S. Department of State, February 10.

Exchange Rate Arrangements and Exchange Restrictions (1997). Washington, D.C.: IMF.

Hamilton, M. (1998). "The Last Great Race for Oil Revenue?" *Washington Post*, April 26.

Huntington, S. (1997). *Clash of Civilizations: The Remaking of World Order*. New York: Touchstone.

International Financial Statistics (1997). Washington, D.C.: IMF.

Kaser, M. (1997). "Economic Transition in Six Central Asian Economies." *Central Asian Survey* 16:1.

Mark, D. (1997). "Eurasia Letter: Russia and the New Transcaucasus." *Foreign Policy*, Winter 1996–97, 141–159.

Moody's International Manual (1996). New York: Vicki Pearthree Raeburn Publishers.

"OECD-Turkish Stability" (1998). *Turkish Times*, April 15.

Pearl, D. (1998). "Rial Problems: Economic Woes Complicate Any Thaw with the U.S." *Wall Street Journal*, June 19.

Pomfret, R. (1997). "The Economic Cooperation Organization: Regional Forum or Irrelevant Talking Shop?" *Caspian Crossroads*, Spring.

Tarock, A., and A. Sewy (1997). "Iran's Policy in Central Asia." *Central Asian Survey* 16:2.

Temple, M. (1994). *Regional Economics.* London: St. Martin's Press.

World Development Report (WDR) (1995, 1997, 1999). World Bank. New York: Oxford University Press.

9

The Export Prospects of Iran: An Analysis of a Country under U.S. Sanctions

The essence of formulating an export strategy is in relating the country's national and industrial resources, capabilities, and constraints to developing its core export competencies, relating core competencies to the achievement of competitive advantages leading to competitive export strategies. Although the identification of competitive advantage is broad, encompassing social as well as economic forces, the key aspect is in fully understanding the nature of the global competitive environment as it relates to trade. Forces outside the country are significant. While these forces affect all countries and industries, the key for Iran is in its ability to relate its competencies—industrial, national, and otherwise—by taking advantage of the global opportunities. The chapter analyzes the structural framework of Iran's exports.

This chapter will also assess Iran's foreign trade in the post-revolution era in the three major dimensions: the growth in the volume of trade and variations in the balance of trade, changes in the composition of trade, and shifts in the direction of trade. Problems and prospects of foreign trade of non-oil products receive particular attention.

Moreover the chapter will examine the changing international environment, including the political, cultural, and economic scenes, as it relates to determining trends and potential export opportunities.

Table 9.1: Foreign Trade			
	1996	1997	1998
Oil exports (MB/d)	2.5	2.55	2.6
Oil output (MB/d)	3.6	3.6	3.6
Oil and gas exports ($ml)	15,141	18, 500	18,000
Non-oil exports ($ml)	3,234	3,000	3,000
Total exports	18,375	21,500	21,000
Imports ($ml)	12,678	15,000	15,000
Trade balance (fob)	5,697	6,500	6,000

Source: Compiled from various issues of *OPEC Bulletin*, Vienna, Austria.

INTRODUCTION

Since slashing imports in 1994, Iran has been running large surpluses on its balance of payments. The trade surplus averaged about $6 billion in the past two years, and the current account surplus averaged well above $4 billion. By March 20, 1997, the trade surplus was around $6.5 billion, which has allowed for easy foreign debt service of about $5 billion per year. Non-oil goods export revenues, which were expected to reach well over $4 billion per year, have since fallen by about one-quarter. (See Tables 9.1, 9.2.)

The largely unilateral move toward trade liberalization in Iran observed since the end of the Iran-Iraq War represents an effective shift in development strategy from import substitution (self-sufficiency) to an export-oriented (export-promoting) framework, which has been partially responsible for higher growth rates. At the same time, it has required a well defined export strategy in a competitive environment.

STRATEGIC DIMENSIONS OF IRAN'S EXPORTS

The country-specific advantage that Iran's export strategies can concentrate on must include a holistic strategic posture along the following dimensions:

1. Strategy as a means of establishing the country's objectives in terms of its long-term goals and resource allocations. Only a change internally or externally (in the environment) can call for a reexamination of the objectives and subsequent adjustment of the strategy. An erratic change of strategic direction would be extremely distractive to everyone involved—

Table 9.2: Selected Economic Indicators			
	1996	1997	1998
Current account ($ml)	3,478	4,000	3,000
GDP growth (%)	3.5	5.0	4.0
Inflation (%)	50	25	25

Sources: *MEED*, February 10, 1997, and *World Development Report*, Washington, D.C.: World Bank, 1999.

the export firms, the workers, and managers. It is crucial to align the country's bureaucracy, human resources, financial, legal, and technological and physical resources with the goals and objectives.

2. Identification of the country's export competitive advantage(s):

   a. What can the country export well?

   b. In what areas should it not commit any resources?

   c. What export activities should the country be in that it currently is not?

   d. What is the country likely to benefit from exporting?

   e. What resources should be invested in heavily? The labor force? Technology? etc.

3. Strategy as a way to define the tasks to be performed by the government, private sector, and others. Harmonization and coordination between appropriate government agencies and business.

4. Strategy as a response to external competition, threats, and attacks, as well as to external opportunities and internal strengths and weaknesses to achieve export competitiveness.

5. Strategy as a way to define and deal with the allocation of success. How will the country allocate the benefits of a successful export-oriented strategy?

From these dimensions, the strategy becomes a fundamental framework through which the country can assert itself in a changing geo-economic global environment. The only way to make all of the competing elements consistent and cooperative is to establish a sense of permanent strategic direction, with a sense of strategic intent.

DETERMINING FACTORS

In determining Iran's competitive position in non-oil, noncommodity, manufacturing, or service industries, such as autos, petrochemicals, textiles and steel, decorative tile and stone, and software, one must be aware of the global market, a firm's position in the industry, and the industry's stage of development, as well as the product's particular stage in its life cycle. This must be analyzed, globally as well as regionally or country-specifically, depending on the firm's strategic approach and desire to take advantage of economies of scale or scope.

Competition in any of these global industries is intense. The firm's and industry's ability to respond to the intensity of rivalry relies on the soundness of its evaluation of the industry structure, identification of important players in the industry, the role and position of different players, their capabilities, the tangible and intangible resources available to them, as well as the strategic outlook of the key players and trends in the industry. Another factor is the general tradability of product, which is often influenced by industry or local responsiveness. Also, the bargaining power of buyers and product substitutability drive and often determine the ability of firms to maintain their competitive position while remaining profitable (Porter, 1980).

These above mentioned forces jointly influence the intensity of each industry's competition and profitability. It is the configuration of the forces that determines the potential prosperity of selected industries. Iranian firms will have to account for the following forces and set appropriate strategies to position themselves globally.

Any assessment of the importance of external competitive forces would be facilitated by identifying the current major markets for Iranian exports, since this is where the analysis should also focus. Tables 9.3 and 9.4 show the direction (value) and share of Iran's exports to various destinations—all OECD countries, OECD countries in Europe, North America, and other country groups. These figures clearly show the current importance of OECD markets for Iran; in fact, it indicates that Iran is primarily dependent on OECD markets and that it may be negatively affected by changes in accessing the markets. Nearly 70 percent of Iran's exports go to the OECD countries. Of that amount, about 70 percent goes to three countries, Germany, France, Italy. However, once petroleum products are excluded, the importance of these countries changes dramatically—Iran accounts for 23 percent of all regional exports to the OECD.

The importance of European markets for Iranian trade prospects is clear. As such, developments relating to trade barriers should receive priority attention. Since North America receives a negligible percent

Table 9.3: Iran's Selected Trade Indicators					
Geographic Destination of Iran's Exports, 1993					
World ($ million)	OECD Markets (%)	Europe (%)	North America (%)	Japan (%)	Other Countries (%)
15,762.3	68.1	53.4	1.9	16.1	31.9
Product Composition of Iran's Global Exports, as a Percentage of Exports (non-oil)					
All Foods	Agriculture Materials	Fuels	Ores and Metals	All Manufactures, including Carpets	Transport and Machinery
2.5	0.9	92.5	0.3	3.7	0.1

Values of Iran's Exports to OECD (U.S. $ million)				Share of Regional Exports to OECD (%)			
1970	1980	1986	1992	1970	1980	1986	1992
2,131.3	10,781	5,637	10,925	19.0	6.9	9.4	10.2
Non-Energy Goods (U.S. $ million)				Share of Regional Exports to OECD (%)			
248.9	878.9	760.4	1,406.0	13.8	8.9	5.2	4.9

Value of Intra-Regional Exports (U.S. $ million)			Share of All Intraregional (%)		
1970	1980	1990	1970	1980	1990
2,454.8	851.3	734.6	72.2	5.1	8.3

Methodological notes: In 1980 and 1990 Iran failed to report trade statistics. Partner-country statistics have been used to estimate exports.

Source: Statistics compiled from UNCTAD *Handbook of International Trade and Development Statistics*, 1993, or United Nations Statistical Office, COMTRADE.

of Iran's total exports, it is unlikely that changes in the trade policies of NAFTA will have important, direct implications for Iran.

GLOBAL MARKET ENTRY: FIRM SPECIFIC ISSUES AND CONCERNS

The ability of Iranian firms to compete outside the country is tested not only by domestic environmental forces constraining the departure but also by national market-entry barriers. It is more seriously challenged by a firm's place in its industry—the threats it poses to the existing players and the threatened position it will find itself in. Iran's export incentives, promotions, and industrial policy need to identify industries with acceptable entry barriers coupled with low levels of retaliation from the existing competitors.

Table 9.4: Main Trading Partners (% of total by dollar value; calendar years)					
	1989	1990	1991	1992	1993
Exports to:					
Japan	14	20	16	15	15
France	8	8	7	6	9
Italy	6	9	9	9	8
Netherlands	8	6	7	8	7
Belgium-Luxemburg	9	6	6	6	3
Brazil	3	6	6	7	2
Imports from:					
Germany	16	18	20	24	17
Japan	7	11	14	12	10
Italy	6	8	9	10	9
UAE	7	7	5	5	7
UK	4	5	4	5	5
France	2	4	4	3	5

Notes: Germany includes only West Germany until 1990.
  Percentages are rounded up to the next whole number.
Source: IMF, *Direction of Trade Statistics Handbook*, various issues.

With an average growth rate of 6 percent over the past twelve years (compared with growth rate of 0.9 percent in the service sector over the same period) manufacturing (the fastest-growing sector), appears to be a logical sector candidate for export considerations. With a share of 4 percent of exports, manufacturing constitutes the second-highest share after oil and gas and other minerals (*WDR*, 1995).

The Major Sources of Entry Barriers

A firm that enjoys domestic economies of scale, enjoys scale production, produces excess products, and is in the production of price-sensitive products, may be best positioned to use price strategy to enter markets and obtain market share. Examples of such industries at the present time include steel, tires, and pharmaceuticals. However, these industries appear to be location sensitive. Tradability and integration of the firm, either through strategic international alliances or other mechanisms, must be an issue to consider.

Pricing strategy as an entry mode may be appropriate for Iranian firms, provided the firm is able to sustain massive initial costs. In other words, the firm must project the benefits of economies of scale and utilize a pricing strategy the benefits of which may be realized some time in the future. Iranian firms may have a competitive advantage in this regard. However, a pricing strategy is at best precarious if utilized only as a one-dimensional strategy, without any complementary component, since it can trigger an industrywide price war, driving all players to minimize profitability. Iranian firms may be able to have a free ride by identifying markets and industries where expansion is occurring, and by monitoring competitors' volume of advertising, which often enlarges the share of the market for all players. Smaller firms can utilize this opportunity without the added cost (Root, 1994).

Product Differentiation

In the area of product differentiation, brand name, and customer intimacy, Iranian firms face unusual disadvantages in the more mature markets, where brand recognition is often a determining factor for product acceptability. This is partly exacerbated by the lack of long-term experience of most Iranian firms in global marketing, and negative country-of-origin association.

Iranian firms attempting to capture foreign market share based on product differentiation must be willing to commit substantial efforts and resources in the initial stages of market penetration. The firms who adopt a geographic focus along with product differentiation in the newly independent states (NIS) can serve as stepping stones, since few foreign or domestic firms enjoy long-term brand recognition and customer loyalty in those markets. Utilizing product differentiation as a means of industry entrance will by nature become promotion intensive and potentially costly, although this point is very much industry and market sensitive.

Switching Cost

One of the barriers to export is often the "switching cost" the consumer must endure to adapt to a new or different product. Iranian exports must be prepared to meet this challenge. This aspect of export relates to the stage of a particular industry's evolution in the country. Suitable markets would be those that are fundamentally similar, so as not to create significant interruption in the market or lead to product disfunctionality. However, while the level of industry evolution may be of relevance, the overall level of economic development of the country is not. In fact, disparity in this regard can extend the product life cycle.

Switching costs include employee training, expenses related to learning curves, the experience needed to optimize product performance, and time and expenses associated with technical support. Identification of target markets and market segments must include markets where the exporter is able and willing to absorb part of the consumer's switching cost while remaining competitive and profitable. For example, in expanding Iran's handmade carpets abroad, the necessities of proper care, repair, and support services becomes crucial for previous nonusers. Switching from machine-made carpets to handmade encounters cost.

Retaliatory Responses

Conditions that can trigger retaliation by foreign firms include:

- Products going against firms with well-established market shares.
- Firms with well-established local governmental connections.
- Competition in slow-market-growth areas or in an industry in decline. (This may be global or country specific. Industry decline provides opportunity to drive competitors to the competitive floor, where the rate of return on investment becomes negative.)

The level of competition normally intensifies when firms believe that the opportunity to improve their position has arrived (Porter, 1986).

RECOMMENDED STRATEGIES: INDUSTRY SPECIFIC FACTORS

For any recommendation to be implementable and meaningful, the following factors must be considered:

1. Industry growth/decline. (An accurate assessment of the industry stage of development can provide vital insight as to how firms need to position themselves against competitors to obtain and maintain a competitive advantage. For example, the auto industry is faced with a ten-million-unit surplus capacity by the year 2000. About six million of this overcapacity is in the European Union, four million in North America, and the remaining scattered in other parts of the world. This will lead to intense completion, requiring greater degree of product differentiation and product lines while pushing prices down—this in a $200 billion industry.)

2. Industry concentration/fragmentation. (Industry concentration and balance of power among the players significantly influences firm profitability and market share. Using the automobile example, the industry seems to be moving toward greater concentration, mergers, and joint ventures, further restricting access.)

3. Industry resource/factor sensitivity (e.g., automobile industry's high degree of management and technology intensity).

GOVERNMENT AS A FORCE IN EXPORT PROMOTION

Government is recognized as having the potential to influence exports, directly or indirectly, by providing incentives or disincentives. In many Iranian firms and industries with export potential, the government is a major buyer of their output, leaving little or no excess product capacity for exports. For example, in infrastructural-related industries, such as construction, cement, etc., the government's role as a supplier of raw material or other key resources has determined, and continues to determine, who gets what, when, how, how much, and at what price. This is usually done for domestic political reasons rather than any real economic considerations. Government regulations have frequently set limits on domestic firms' ability to engage in international trade. The Iranian government, however, is strongly promoting agriculture exports through a variety of price subsidies or cheaper fertilizers.

No analysis of Iran's export potential is complete without a thorough assessment of the government's present and future policy impacting the structural conditions of trade at all levels (see Table 9.5).

Table 9.5: Main Non-Oil Exports By Type ($ million)					
	1989/90	1990/91	1991/92	1992/93	1993/94
Agricultural and Traditional Goods					
Carpets	345	510	1,162	1,106	1,384
Fresh and Dry Fruits	319	333	532	578	675
Leather	95	57	77	78	115
Caviar	36	44	35	31	32
Other	100	100	100	200	300
Total Agricultural and Traditional Goods	895	1,039	1,938	1,996	2,516
Metal Ores	27	32	51	21	39
Industrial Goods					
Chemicals	34	16	40	18	30
Textiles	5	12	24	56	36
Construction Materials	6	4	5	5	6
Refined Copper	17	77	83	132	140
Steel and Other	61	133	508	759	980
Total Industrial Goods	123	242	660	970	1,192

Note: The figures are rounded up to the next whole number.
Source: Bank Markazi Iran

DISINCENTIVES

Export disincentives are self-imposed policy deterrents to exports. Export disincentives represent a form of trade policy: they make a distinction at the border. Sales to foreign customers are treated differently from sales to domestic customers. Policies that impose barriers to exports do not exist domestically. An example is an export control. Iran's export controls are severe compared to those of its major trading partners, and its export-promotion programs are weak as well. Therefore, export disincentives can be further defined as policy choices that either deter exports or fail to encourage exports. For example, Iran's exports significantly declined and export controls skyrocketed during the eight-year Iran-Iraq War. More than half of all

Iranian-made products required validated licenses, most frequently on a product-specific basis.

Export controls have historically been implemented through licensing requirements and procedures administered variously, and sometimes simultaneously, by the ministry of commerce and customs bureau. Exporting firms have been forced to undergo costly expenditures just to obtain export permission. All Iranian-made exports require some sort of license, not always easy to obtain. Other countries in the region have enforced similar export controls at some point, but Iran exercises tighter controls than do its export competitors.

Inadequate official support of exports is an indirect export disincentive. It can deter potential exports, though not actually banning them. The two most important facets of official export support are export finance and export promotion, partly to offset a negative balance of trade.

Other categories of disincentives can be identified. One would be policies or actions that contribute to the shrinkage of distribution of Iranian-made products abroad, primarily due to the negative associations of the product's country of origin. The most extreme example is a foreign boycott of all or certain Iranian-made products. This has usually occurred in response to a foreign policy posture of the government. Currently, for example, the U.S. embargo against Iran can be cited, as well as milder foreign retaliation against Iranian exports.

COST-INFLICTING EXPORT DISINCENTIVES

These are costs that raise the cost of exporting. One of the most important is the cost of maintaining staff and associated infrastructure to simply deal with paperwork and bureaucracy—to apply for and obtain licenses, maintain records, and so on. Such administrative costs would not be incurred if a firm sold only to domestic buyers, and they are not borne by important Iranian competitors such as in India, Turkey, and many of the Central Asian NISs. It is often argued by Iranian firms that such administrative costs are higher and more burdensome in Iran than virtually anywhere else in the region. Another obvious disincentive is the cost of foreign-exchange market transactions. Furthermore, the relatively heavy Iranian income tax serves as a disincentive.

Empirical studies in other countries indicate that demand-constricting export disincentives are for various reasons more potent in discouraging exports than are cost-constricting disincentives. There are fixed costs, such as overhead for bureaucratic red tape, and variable costs, of variable exchange rates. Fixed-cost export disincentives raise artificial entry barriers for new exports. They appear to be more important than variable costs. More established export firms know the ropes, are typically larger, and are more comfortable with the existing constraints. As a result the threat of entry is perceived as high, diminishing the number of potential exporters (Richardson, 1993).

Another very important category of export disincentive includes import barriers that can function as export disincentives. Well over half of Iran's imports are industrial or capital equipment, such as machine tools; an unknown percentage of manufacturing import categories are components and parts rather than finished products. Limiting imports can reduce industrial output and overall production at the firm and national level. Studies indicate that between two similar economies, the one with both higher imports and exports is more prosperous (Bertsch and Elliot-Gower, 1992).

A final export disincentive is a country's customs infrastructure. Issues include the length and hours of operations; night closures, which can lead to higher transportation costs; unpredictable delays at the borders, which can interfere with the just-in-time inventory needs of foreign importers; and general technological inadequacies and management practices.

Frequent changes in the laws and regulations increases uncertainty and perceived risks to the exporter. This is reflective of a lack of coordinated efforts to put in place long-term export strategies.

POLICY OPTIONS, RECOMMENDATIONS, AND CONCLUSIONS

Iranians are more concerned than they used to be about the country's international competitiveness, but Iran's policies often seem unduly reactive and focused on imports, or inadequately proactive or export oriented.

There are several important general conclusions from the study:

• Iran's policies often prevent strong export performance, sometimes by design, sometimes incidentally. One can guesstimate that in the postwar era

Iran has foregone about $10–12 billion annually because of the policies covered here.

- Demand-constraining export disincentives are more potent than cost-inflicting export disincentives (such as regulatory burdens). Export disincentives that limit demand are more potent than those that merely inhibit it (such as inadequate official support for export finance). Export disincentives that inflict fixed costs, such as legal/administrative staff and support for export licensing, and are more potent than those that inflict variable costs (such as transportation).

POLICY IMPLICATIONS

These recommendations are aimed at reducing the economic cost of export disincentives, relative to some desired level of effectiveness in achieving the objectives that the disincentives were set up to meet. Assessing the net national benefit of export disincentives requires a separate study.

- The Export Promotion Office needs to be strengthened with executive authority to coordinate all export-promotion programs nationally. The office should have authority to enforce cooperation.
- There should be annual reports, prepared by an appropriate agency of the government, on the quantitative effects of export controls on the country's export competitiveness. Such reports should follow a scientific methodology, including sectoral and product-specific analyses, and they should attempt to assess the effects of export controls on foreign direct investment in the country.
- Official export-finance programs must be supplemented to make capital goods and services competitive in financial terms with those of foreign competitors, especially in projects where private financial markets are inadequate—for example, public infrastructure in neighboring countries or the NISs of central Asia. Recent economic pacts and trade understandings allow domestic firms to participate in these markets.
- Finally, it is important to note that official export-promotion programs seem to have little quantitative impact on Iran's exports, however valuable their contributions to export consciousness-raising.

Disincentives may also have another unintentional side effect, of raising entry barriers for smaller firms, which can lead to a concentration of larger exporters and fewer firms, reducing the overall level of competition, performance, and economic benefits of exporting at all levels.

REFERENCES

Bertsch, G., and S. Elliot-Gower (1992). *Export Controls in Transition: Perspectives, Problems and Prospects.* Durham, N.C.: Duke University Press.

Grant, R. (1996). *Contemporary Strategy Analysis.* Oxford: Blackwell.

Hax, A., and S. Majluf (1996). *The Strategy Concept and Process: A Pragmatic Approach.* Englewood Cliffs, N.J.: Prentice Hall.

Jackson, J. (1995). *The World Trading System.* Cambridge, Mass.: MIT Press.

Johnson, T. (1997). *Export/Import.* New York: Amacom.

Porter, M. (Ed.) (1986). *Competition in Global Industries.* Boston: Harvard Business School Press.

———. (1980). *Competitive Strategy.* New York: Free Press.

Richardson, D. (1993). *Sizing Up U.S. Export Disincentives.* Washington, D.C.: Institute for International Economics.

Root, F. (1994). *Entry Strategies for International Markets.* New York: Lexington.

Schott, J. J. (1994). *The Uruguay Round.* Washington, D.C.: Institute for International Economics.

World Development Report (WDR) (1995, 1999). Washington, D.C.: World Bank.

10

Agriculture Policy and Prospects in Iran: An Overview

This chapter is concerned with the production and trading of agricultural products in Iran. It analyzes the development of the agricultural sector of the economy of Iran from 1980 to the present day. In the process, it shows long-term trends in the production and trade of all agricultural products. This review will attempt to show trends that have occurred in Iran in the postrevolutionary period. One is the rise in the level of agricultural products; however, the increase in the production has not kept pace with a substantial rise in population, leading to increased imports of all categories of agricultural products. Iran, once an exporter, is now a net importer of agricultural products. This chapter will also examine how Iran is now seeking to develop its agricultural sector, and to what extent it has been successful.

OVERVIEW

Rapid changes are evident in the operation of farms in Iran and in the ways in which farmers operate their farms. Key determinants of these changes are migration and modernization, but responsibility falls also on major new developments in other aspects of agricultural production, marketing, and trade. The first Iranian five-year developmental plan increased involvement of state agencies in agricultural and rural change, and it directed some of this involvement toward the modernization of farming practices. This progressive trend has brought a number of practices, from mechanization to the provision of fertilizers and new seed types to irrigation, as well as a variety of infrastructural projects, including roads. At the same time, Iranian agriculture has moved still farther from a locally oriented system toward integration into a nationwide commercial network.

Most important of all have been the changes in the makeup of the Iranian rural community itself. Many people have left their villages for Iran's cities or were forced off their farms by the eight-year war with Iraq. Moreover, nonfarming activity is increasingly in evidence in villages and rural areas. Still, agriculture remains the largest employment sector, with 45 percent of the labor force (including livestock rearing and fishing) in 1990, compared with nearly 36 percent in 1980. In 1989, Iran's total population amounted to about fifty-five million, twenty-nine million of which were urban dwellers, with the remaining twenty-six million residing in the rural parts. This is an increase in rural population to about 48 percent of the total population. This amounts to an average population growth rate in the rural areas of about 2.5 percent. In the rural areas, about 57 percent of the labor force is engaged in farming. About 57 percent of this agriculture labor force are men; 32 percent of the women in rural areas have unearned income as housewives. This is in addition to those unemployed or actively seeking jobs, who total more than 5 percent. These figures, however clear, fail to reflect the growing number of farmers and farm workers who now work only "part time" in agriculture, either because they are developing other skills in the village or because they spend most of their time away from home as migrant workers. The population now exceeds sixty million.

The very highest level of socio-economic development is associated with Iran's four major urban areas—Tehran, Mashad, Tabriz, and Isphahan. These cities are now linked to each other, and to middle-rank and smaller towns across the country, by a network of roads, overcoming the deterioration in the rail system and intercity air service that has contributed to the current insufficient infrastructure of communications and transportation. Thousands of villages are now linked to nearby market towns by roads, with truck or bus service. Some of these local roads have cut journeys that once to took hours to minutes.

Indeed, the movement of people has, arguably, become the principal factor affecting Iranian agriculture and the rural people on whom it depends. Migration, rural-urban and international, has significant demographic implications. It is clear that more than a third of Iran's districts or subprovinces (*Shahrestan*) were losing rural people during the 1980s. By 1990, 10 percent of the districts in the country were reporting a net loss of rural people—although birth rates remained high. Most of these districts are located in the border area with Iraq, but some are on the Persian Gulf coast, and some are in Iran's Baluchestan corner. During the 1980s, a number of provinces began to show net losses in urban as well as rural population. Between 1980 and 1990, however, there was an increase in the total population in five of Iran's provinces. Other provinces gained population by migration. All but two of these are in the western half of the country and four are some of the largest Iranian provinces, wherein urban growth has been at its most dramatic. In the capital, Tehran, for example, about 40 percent of the present inhabitants were born outside the province—most of those are rural and small-town Iranians living in modest conditions. An estimated third of Iran's sixty million inhabitants live below the poverty line, many without basic sanitation. Some indication of trends in the overall standard of living of farmers and city dwellers in the country is shown in Table 10.5.

Few immigrants from farming backgrounds can easily find full employment in the formal economies of the cities. Many remain unemployed at best. Sometimes groups move together into a city, perhaps from a single village. Links with the home village or small town persist: money may be sent home and visits made. Such links may be critical to the maintenance of relatives in rural areas, especially where local resources are not meeting aspirations. These links and the attitudes developing along with them contribute to the qualitative change that is taking place in rural, as well as urban, Iran. The farmer now often feels that he is part of a national-urban-rural society rather than of the narrower horizons that confined his parents. Added to the personal ties rural citizens have to relatives who have left farming—or to the subsidies that are sent back—are the links that are now possible through media-agriculture extension and other branches of state services. As a result of the development of a variety of urban-rural links, more of Iran's sixty-five thousand villages are now market seeking, in that they show signs of losing their strictly "village" status.

FARM MECHANIZATION

One of the most visible changes in Iranian agriculture in the 1970s and 1980s was the appearance of tractors and other farm machines as replacements for the traditional uses of animals, people, and old-style implements and techniques. Whereas in 1968 the government projected sale of a thousand tractors, and in 1975 there were fewer than 10,900 tractors built in the whole of Iran, in 1983 there were more than 1,500; by 1988 the number had reached five thousand. Other machinery, such as spray pumps, topped thirty-two thousand that year. Between 1975 and 1983 there was a 1.5-fold increase in the number of tractors; a study by the ministry of agriculture in 1989 projected a need for almost 40,300 tractors nationwide.

In 1986 mechanization had reached a point where the Iranian Corporation for the Development of Agricultural Machinery was publishing studies of mechanization in different provinces. For example, these studies revealed that in the province of Isphahan (one of the larger agriculture provinces), only 30 percent of available agricultural machinery was effectively utilized. In the 1980s, production of machines within the country was increasingly faced with bottlenecks, due to an eight-year war with Iraq and shortages of foreign exchange.

The farm mechanization experienced in Iran can be described as at best haphazard. During the first rush to mechanize, the importation of farm machines—especially tractors—was often ad hoc and uncoordinated. Different makes of machines would arrive in a village, presenting the problem incompatible spare parts and specialist servicing and repair. Moreover, rural roads were frequently quite unsuitable for unmanageably large tractors, which could, during transit, demolish field and terrace walls, with consequent soil loss. Yet despite difficulties of cost and maintenance, the tractor was seen not only as a means of working more land for one's own account but also as a basis for extra earnings through leasing to others. Machines have been more than mere farm implements, for they signal higher socioeconomic status and provide a focus for investment for rural Iran.

The extent to which machines have contributed to the migration of rural people is debatable; certainly, at the least, machines have increased productivity. For example, to plow a hectare of land takes on average about 1.3 minutes with an average tractor, versus 5.4 minutes with cow-drawn plows. Further, the nature of mechanized agricultural implements is such that they work more efficiently on larger and less fragmented holdings than those characteristic of traditional agricultural practice in Iran. In 1982, about 90 percent of farms were under twenty-five hectares; these constituted more than 76 percent of total farmlands. Thus, the foundation of the traditional

Table 10.1: Farm Size								
	1974				1982-1983			
Farm Categories	Farms (in 1,000s)	(%)	Area of Land (in hectares)	(%)	Farms (in 1,000s)	(%)	Area of Land (in hectares)	(%)
Total Farmland	2,480	100	16,417	100	2,656	100	13,079	100
Under 1 Hectare*	734	29.5	260	1.6	863	32.5	307	2.3
1 to 2 Hectares	322	13	444	2.7	407	15.3	553	4.2
2 to 5 Hectares	542	21.9	1,733	10.6	624	23.5	1,992	15.2
5 to 10 Hectares	428	17.3	2,952	18	408	15.4	2,806	21.4
10 to 50 Hectares	428	17.3	7,501	45.7	339	12.8	5,693	43.5
50 to 100 Hectares	16	0.6	1,074	6.5	11	0.4	718	5.5
100 Hectares +	10	0.4	2,454	14.9	4	0.1	1,009	7.7

Note: A hectare is = 10,000 meters.

Sources: Organization of Planning and Budget, State Institute of Statistics–Agricultural Statistics, Census 1974, March 1974; Organization of Planning and Budget, State Institute of Statistics–Agricultural Statistics, Census 1982–1983, March 1983.

Iranian agro-economy is based on small farms, a situation at odds with modernization through mechanization, as shown in Table 10.1.

Between 1972 and 1982, the area under the plow (whether animal or tractor) in Iran decreased from 17.2 million hectares to 15 million hectares. This trend continued up to 1985 and then stabilized at about 14 million hectares, even as production remained constant. In 1974, total farmland was calculated at about 13 million hectares; there were then two tractors for every thousand hectares. This ratio reached 3.6 tractors per thousand hectares by 1980. In 1982 there were 93,051 tractors used in farming.

Between 1982 and 1990, a total of 92,800 tractors were distributed among farmers by the Corporation for Development of Agricultural Machinery. The number of tractors distributed decreased from 25,000 in 1982 to about 2,500 in 1990. Taking into account both the number of tractors taken out of circulation and those in use during that period, the number of tractors per hectare remained constant. It is interesting to note that in 1982, tractors were used in 96 percent of farms of less than twenty five hectares, 80 percent of ten-hectare farms, 58 percent of farms less than five hectares, and 28 percent of farms under two hectares. Farms larger than twenty-five

Table 10.2: Average Growth Rate	
(1980-1987)	% Change
Wheat	3.1
Barley	10.3
Rice	5.4
Sugarbeets	2.1
Cotton	0.8
Vegetable Oil	-2.4
Red Meat (beef)	2.6
White Meat (poultry)	4.3
Chicken Eggs	-1
Milk	3.2

Source: Ministry of Agriculture.

hectares were using tractors at a rate of 3.4 each in 1982. These figures, with little variation, hold true for other sorts of farm machinery.

AGRICULTURE PRODUCTIVITY

Let us now turn to the output of all this agricultural endeavor. Wheat, Iran's principal agricultural product, has shown a nearly 3 percent increase in output following the revolution of 1980. Other crops have increased even more: barley, rice, sugarbeets, and cotton are examples, as are beef and poultry, with 2.6 percent and 4.3 percent increases, respectively. Figures for selected farm products since 1980 are shown in Table 10.2.

Recent increases in the output of field crops have been offset by a population growth rate of about 3.7 percent. Agricultural value-added in the years from 1983 to 1986 stood at 12 percent, 13 percent, 14 percent, and 19 percent respectively.

While Iran's agricultural sector and such directly related industries as animal husbandry (i.e., slaughter houses, meat preservation, and flour preparation) contribute significantly to the agricultural sector, little trickle-down affects the rest of the economy. Arguably, the agricultural sector as it now stands in Iran cannot be effectively utilized as an engine of economic growth and development. The agricultural

Table 10.3: Number of Selected Livestock in Iran, 1988-1989 (in thousands)	
Sheep/Lamb	36,590
Goat/Baby Goat	21,440
Cow & Native Calf	5,113
Bred Cow	155
Cow (other)	250
Buffalo	439
Camel	105
Horse/Mule	423
Donkey	2,176

Source: Ministry of Agriculture, Division of Livestock and Birds.

sector has not been able to expand other sectors, such as railroad transport, the auto industry, or communication, nor has it been able to provide the impetus for an information industry in the country, as it did, for example, in the United States at the turn of the century.

At the present time, there is a total of five hundred veterinarians and five thousand veterinary technicians in Iran. If accurate, the ratio of trained personnel to livestock is sufficient to take care of about 30 million livestock, whereas, the livestock population surpasses 120 million, which means about 75 percent of the livestock is deprived of trained personnel. Some indication of trends in the overall numbers of farm animals in the country is shown in Table 10.3. The total number of public-sector personnel involved in livestock and animal husbandry is 270 technicians, four hundred veterinarians, and two technicians for every ten thousand head.

Moreover, animals suffering from disease exceeded six million in 1985, compared to one million in 1979, which means that there has been an increase of 250,000 diseased livestock annually. The diseased animals contributed to a 27 percent reduction in milk production and 35 percent in wool.

Iran, with an area of 1,648,000 square kilometers, has a total of 17 million hectares of farmland (20 percent of the country), of which about 32 percent, or 5.5 million hectares is not cultivated. Of the 11.5 million under cultivation, about 50 percent, or 5.6 million hectares, is irrigated, including one million hectare in trees. The largest area cultivated is in wheat, followed by barley.

Total family farms in the country add up to about 3,390,000, with

Table 10.4: Regional Shares in Total Annual Production and Area Utilized			
Region	Production (tons)	Area (hectares)	#(1000s)
Fars	35,000 lamb 20,000 beef	350	1,200 lamb 100 cow
Moghan	40,000 lamb 20,000 beef	44,000	1,500 lamb 100 cow
Azerbaijan, Fars, Gillan, Kermanshah	30,000 milk	N/A	N/A
Tehran	500 milk daily	N/A	N/A
Others	30,000 lamb and beef	N/A	500 lamb 100 cow

Source: Ministry of Agriculture, Milk/Meat Collectives, 1988–1989.

an average of about six hectares of farmland each. This is an increase of two hectares from the beginning of the revolution and a threefold increase from pre–oil embargo year of 1973. Based on some studies, about 30 percent of Iranian agriculture products never make it to the market. In addition to diseased crops, this is due to shortcomings in distribution.

Regional contrasts have persisted in Iran, as shown in Table 10.4. Three zones in Iran—the Caspian Sea, Persian Gulf, and Khorason—have generally retained their leads over the Fars interior and the eastern uplands in levels of development in general and in average income in particular. But certain advantaged areas stand out: the grain-growing plains of inland Khtizestan and those parts of the center and east that have been able to benefit from irrigation schemes in the Seefed Rud area are examples. Certainly the breakdown of Iran into supposedly richer western and poorer eastern halves, which has figured in much thinking about the development of the country, is as misleading as before. The real pattern is more complex, with patches of backwardness in the west, relatively advanced areas in the east.

As to the environment, the patterns of agriculture in Iran reflect the country's varied landscape and climate. The Persian Gulf and the Gulf of Oman areas have hot, dry summers and mild, wet winters. The Caspian Sea zone is less mild, but its precipitation is greater throughout the year. The interior plateau and eastern uplands are cut off from much of the moderating maritime influence by mountain ranges—the Zagrous in the west and the Alborz in the north. This mountain rim and the eastern highlands are better watered because of their height but are cold in winter, especially in the north. Traditionally, the interior of the Iranian plateau has depended on seasonally rain-fed farming, while the southern and western edges have been able to develop irrigation in response to summer droughts. A major challenge to Iranian agriculture policy is to extend the irrigable area. This, together with other development in the structure and support of Iranian agriculture, should reduce its vulnerability to the elements.

AGRICULTURAL TRADE

Despite initiatives by the state, individual enterprise, and the expansion of arable area, the relative position of Iran's agriculture has slipped. Farm-product exports decreased by about 85 percent between 1974 and 1981; exports of fresh and dried fruits fell to 33,000 tons in 1981. In 1985, they were creeping up to about 97,000 tons.

It should be noted that the potential capability of dried agriculture products (including fresh and dried dates, grapes and raisins, pistachio and pistachio kernels, and almonds and other traditional dried fruits) is estimated at about 575,000 tons. The potential export capability of such products is at about 210,000 tons. Between 1982 and 1984, production remained below capacity by about 8 percent. Were the production capability of dried fruits and vegetables fully utilized, they could produce an annual billion-dollar export revenue.

Farm products in 1988 accounted for some 95 percent of non-oil exports, including carpets, compared with 3.9 percent for industrial goods (though one-twentieth of these are processed agriculture products); the figures include wool and cotton textiles, synthetic fibers, and medicines. It must be noted also that total non-oil exports account for only about 6 percent of total exports, which is one of the highest among the OPEC members, setting aside Malaysia and Indonesia. Agricultural exports' contribution to national income has fallen consistently, from about 3 percent in 1972 to about 0.2 percent now. Agriculture's contribution to national income has also fallen considerably, from about 9 percent in 1977 to about 7 percent in 1983. In other words, about 48 percent of the population—the rural portion—contributes about 7 percent to national income. Currently, a review of national policy regarding the role of agricultural sector is under way, with implications for its place both in international trade and within the country. The background of this review includes both the recovery of Iran from the worst of its economic problems in the

Table 10.5: Comparative Comfort (%) Level of Farm and City Dwellers				
Category	Piped Water	Electricity	Refrigeration	Television
1977 Farm	11.7	16.2	7.6	3.2
1977 City	79.6	91.6	73	52.2
1982 Farm	32.5	49.1	29.6	19.4
1982 City	93.4	99.4	88.1	75.6

Source: Ministry of Agriculture (1977–1983), *Agriculture Economic Report.*

1980s and the very rapid deterioration of Iranian agricultural infrastructure. Meanwhile, uncertainties about the future have a special relevance to Iran's agriculture (see Table 10.5).

The years 1988–89 marked a low point for the Iranian economy, with oil prices plummeting, an exchange crisis, an escalating rate of inflation, the search for external support from the International Monetary Fund and elsewhere, and then—in summer 1990—a major, devastating earthquake in northern Iran. Now the country's balance of payments is improving; partly in response to the de facto devaluation of Iranian rial and a sharp increase in the price of oil, export earnings are rising impressively (Table 10.6).

The new export opportunities for Iran in the developing countries have helped the country's recovery from its recent economic problems. Trade with Turkey, South Korea, Argentina, and Brazil has increased. Iran and Turkey possess great potential for improving their trade relations, as the economic policies implemented in both countries are bringing a certain degree of dynamism aimed at creating structural changes. In 1987, Iran's imports from South Korea remained unchanged in terms of volume and value, while Iranian exports to South Korea rose to 1,744 tons, with a total value of $3.4 million. Meanwhile the EC and EFTA, which now take more than 50 percent of all of Iran's exports, continue to buy "traditional" luxury foodstuffs (figs, raisins, and pistachios) and industrial crops, such as cotton and oil seeds, but their demand for ordinary foodstuffs has been slow to rise (Table 10.7).

A dilemma of Iranian agriculture is that markets are as hard to penetrate in the Middle East as they are in Europe, if not necessarily for the same reasons. In terms of closer association with the EU, Iran presents a competitive threat in food exports to the community's Mediterranean members. Apart from limited quantities of traditional

| Table 10.6: Iran's Non-Oil Exports (by weight) ||
Year	Weight-ton 1,000
1977	1,138
1978	1,336
1979	579
1980	129
1981	154
1982	162
1983	231
1984	269
1985	526
1986	646

Source: Foreign Trade Statistics, 1977–1986.

sales, such as pistachios, figs, and Persian melons, Iran has not been able significantly to expand exports to Europe; even sectors as these show significant and sharp fluctuations from year to year. In both European and Middle Eastern markets, Iran's prospects for exports of fruit, vegetables, and livestock products will depend in part on improved yield and quality control.

The sudden influx of oil revenues as a consequence of Saddam Hussein's invasion of Kuwait had quite a direct effect on Iranian agriculture. The impact of oil revenues on farming in Iran was evident in three ways: capital, repatriation of skilled Iranian expatriates involved in the field of agriculture, and more general changes in attitudes and aspirations. Money brought back to rural Iran will pay for consumer goods, such as cars and appliances, but it also will provide investment funding in farming itself (machinery, land, livestock, etc.) and in nonfarming enterprises in villages. Along with the growing range of skills in rural areas go changes in the division of labor. Non-wage field work by women and children declines rapidly where machines take over.

Iranian agriculture is changing in response to national as well as individual initiatives. Petrodollars are increasingly important at all levels, but both activity and commitment remain vulnerable to change in the availability of finance. Iranians have no guarantee that revenues will continue to expand as rapidly as they did in the first years of the

Table 10.7: Iran's Exports by Destination	
	% 1980 - 1986
European Union	45.5
EFTA	9.5
South Korea	4.5 (1988)
Turkey	4.5 (1988)
Other	36.0

Source: *Direction of Trade*, Washington D.C.: IMF.

1990s. Exports of agriculture commodities, whether to Europe or to the Middle East, remain vulnerable to competition and to protection. Internally, Iranian agriculture continues to be subject to environmental factors, to changes in development priorities in Tehran, to ramifications of trends at the international level, and to new abilities and aspirations among rural Iranians. Pessimistic forecasters see limits approaching to agricultural expansion in Iran, both in the total area farmed and in extent to which Tehran can influence the progress of that sector.

The Islamic government established in Iran after the 1979 revolution reintroduced planning as a guiding principle in the economy; the state plan and budget organization's first five-year development plan, for 1989–1994, indicated official priorities. It stressed the improvement of technological basis of agriculture. More than 6 percent growth for the agricultural sector was projected under the new plan, 5.3 percent for animal husbandry, nearly 15 percent for forestry, and 28 percent for fisheries. Wheat production was projected to increase by about 10 percent, from 7.012 thousand tons to 11.049 thousand tons in 1994. Further rice production was expected to increase by around 4 percent, from 1.700 thousand tons in 1989 to 2.205 thousand tons in 1994. Such increases required investment outlays totaling more than $12 billion for the agricultural sector. The second and third plans (ending by 2004) essentially provide very similar growth figures.

Nevertheless, Iran remains a net agriculture importer, importing foodstuff worth upward of $400 billion per annum. This is despite early efforts by the Islamic Republic to become self-sufficient. Imports have increased by 80 percent since 1994; Iran is now the region's biggest food buyer. The leading suppliers include Australia, Canada, France, Sweden, Finland, Ukraine, and Kazakhstan.

During the first developmental plan, the emphasis on the main investment priorities was strengthened, with about $7 billion foreign exchange allocation going to water and soil resource developments and to tractors and equipment. The plan stressed improvements in irrigation, some of this in the context of a score of major dams, *qanats*, and water tunnel projects, with multiple regional development aims. The first plan also emphasized a range of yield improvements like new seeds, to reduce the amount of land to be plowed. These were consistent with calls for higher growth rates for both crops and livestock than those achieved previously, though the overriding commitment persisted to economic development based primarily on industrialization. The greatest optimism for export expansion centers on wheat. Somewhat lower growth levels were hoped for in cotton, pistachios, and especially fruit and vegetables, where the scope of improvement is considerable. The plan recognized that agriculture exports faced not only problems of market penetration but also persistent Iranian shortcomings in industrialization, quality control, and coordination of marketing initiatives.

Overall, the national plan envisaged a continuing change in the production mix, away from traditional patterns dominated by subsistence, market-ignoring village farming and toward coordinated, market-seeking, commercial agriculture, providing a basis for agroindustries and expansion. Such a national plan formula in fact recognized what in any case needs to happen in Iranian agriculture—integrated development, with consistent and linked changes in sectors and in demographic and socioeconomic trends.

The principal problem facing the decision makers and planners in Tehran is the movements of people within the country and changes in their expectations, which threaten to overwhelm the efforts of the state. Along with these problems is the reality of an agricultural system in which most production has been in the hands of hundreds of thousands of small-scale producers, while marketing, financial support, and extension services have been developed by a broad structure of governmental agencies and ministries.

Since the 1980s, Iranian farmers have become more accustomed to subsidies and price support, to low-interest credit, and to help from extension services. Taxation has hit them far less harshly than other sectors—notably people in state-service employment. This support role of the state in agriculture is now being questioned and reassessed by policy makers in Tehran, while farmers themselves are developing new demands and expectations. In short, there is a changing state-individual mix in Iranian agriculture, with initiatives and responses on both sides.

A major aspect of state involvement in agricultural development, low-interest credit, has been distributed primarily through small co-operatives, which, it is hoped, will help to maximize the effectiveness of the loans while getting farmers used to formal cooperation itself. The durability of such cooperatives varies greatly, as does the readiness of Iranian farmers to invest in areas preferred by the agriculture bank. Inevitably, cheap credit on such a scale becomes politically sensitive, as entrepreneurs and agriculture products have become elements in the relationship between producer and state—which now increasingly recognizes a need for credit to be set more strictly in regard to domestic and world conditions.

The prominence of tractors and other farm machinery in recent agricultural development in Iran has itself been subject to government import-duty and exchange restrictions. Similarly, the state can manipulate the supply of increasingly popular chemical fertilizers through tax, price support, and credit arrangements.

Some government activity in irrigation expansion in Iran combines credit funding both to farmers for small-scale activities and to major water-development projects. Plan targets called for 6 percent increase in the total arable area to be irrigable by 1994, from 6,300,000 hectares to 6,700,000. Substantial areas of potentially irrigable land, however, await the completion of irrigation works. One problem here, as elsewhere in Iranian agriculture, is the lack of sufficient coordination between state agencies.

The state agricultural extension service has been an important catalyst for change during the past decade. It has had an identity separate from the many other government ministries and agencies responsible for work with farmers in agriculture or related infrastructural developments. Shortcomings of coordination and shortages of the qualified manpower, transport, and equipment have hampered progress. There are less than twelve farm-disease researchers in the public sector in the entire country. They enjoy little support, such as qualified personnel or computer systems. In general, there are less than eighty-two scientific researchers per one million population in the country. The problem of underqualification remains, along with personal reluctance to indulge in field work, continuing vehicle and other short-ages, and the lack of personnel for data collection and other routine research-related tasks. Notwithstanding these limitations, the 1989–94 plan aimed at a further doubling of qualified personnel. Probably the most important problem has been Iranian farmers' lack of aware-ness of the ways in which the state can help them, from the provision of credit or seed for new crop varieties, to pest-control measures or advice on cultivation and marketing.

CONCLUDING REMARKS

In a brief review of the main features of progress in Iranian agri-culture, it is easy to list persistent operational constraints and resource shortages. One can point also to the relative decline of the sector within the national economy. Yet there are positive changes to report. Some subsectors have expanded rapidly; certain export developments in recent years have been rapid and innovative. Still, planned expan-sion rates for field crops, animal husbandry, forestry products, and water schemes have not been achieved in most cases. Ultimately, the most important changes in agriculture in contemporary Iran involve the farmers and stock breeders themselves.

REFERENCES

Agra Europe, August 25, 1995.

Agra Europe, September 20, 1996.

Amuzegar, J. (1993). *Iran's Economy*. London: IB Tauris.

Bhaduri, A., and R. Skarstein (Eds.), (1997). *Economic Development and Agriculture Productivity*. Cheltenham, U.K.: Edward Elgar Publish-ing, Ltd.

MEED, September 5, 1997.

Ministry of Agriculture (1983–1997). *Agriculture Economic Report*. Tehran, Iran.

Sharifi, M. (1998). "The Export Supply Functions of Agriculture Products in Iran: An Estimation." *Iranian Journal of Trade Studies (IJTS) Quarterly* 2:6.

World Development Report (1998). World Bank. New York: Oxford Uni-versity Press.

Yildrim, T., A. Shmitz, and W. H. Furtan (Eds.) (1998). *World Agriculture Trade*. Boulder, Colo.: Westview Press.

Conclusion: The Middle East beyond the Year 2000

The idea of achieving economic development and prosperity in today's Middle East—a region that has attracted the attention of the entire world, and which for hundreds of years has been struggling to modernize—is no doubt difficult.

It is a region whose strategic position and political and economic status make it coveted by the world's business leaders and outside powers, who have always thought of dominating it. To achieve economic development and to pursue international business in a region like the Middle East presents serious issues. This book presents and identifies a number of key socio-economic constants in the Middle East's business environment. The elements of geopolitics, the permanence of geographic, ethnographic, demographic, cultural factors, and religion have all left their mark on the Middle East's approach to the outside world. But no region is purely hostage to such determinants; leadership and the existence of a strategic raw material, oil, have also greatly shaped the business and economic environment in the region.

THE ROLE OF ISLAM

A creative, forward-looking approach to the interpretation of Islam in the contemporary Middle East could ultimately have considerable impact on the business environment. One wonders, however, whether this will happen without a backlash. Yet, success in this area could have a major impact on the overall revitalization of the region, economic development, and the business environment, bringing them into closer alignment with the realities of modern life world-wide.

GLOBALIZATION

Globalization presents both opportunities and threats for the Middle East: opportunities in the sense of economic abundance, freedom of choice, and greater cultural interactions; threats in the form of economic insecurity, political instability, and cultural hegemony. The key agent of globalization is the multinational enterprise (MNE). Spanning the region, their affiliates and strategic alliances linking the countries, multinationals are the embodiments and principal agents of globalization of the region.

The Middle East is a region of gifted people and a superb cultural heritage, capable of great contributions to the global community. The question is whether it can move with new maturity into the future, recognize that international business may now be undergoing a decisive period of change in the post–cold war global age.

As market forces emerge more strongly in this region in the next millennium, the Middle East will be a key player in global business, especially the countries discussed in this book, if differences among these states can be minimized. The Middle East has already set down its marker as an economically viable region in the global economy. Thus, apart from oil, the Middle East will be playing an important role in global business. If the Middle East can move on with economic integration, it will be poised for an activist role in the global marketplace in the next century, ideally one that it will allow for greater integration into the global economy. For the past thirty years the Middle East, witness to three major wars and a revolution, has been synonymous with political turmoil and conflict. The importance of the Middle East was reinforced by the mid-1970s rise in the price of oil, although this also contributed to the region's reputation for instability.

The book provides guidelines by which multinationals can reconcile the opportunities presented in the region with the need for social and economic adjustments to enhance the abilities of enterprises and governments to maximize these opportunities.

The globalization age and the subsequent escalation of competition have had momentous impacts on the socio-economic structure of the region. Internal circumstances have experienced enormous change, propelled by the phenomenal pace of social and economic progress. The region's societies have been dramatically transformed, and the business environment and infrastructure have been developed at an unprecedented speed. While these changes have taken place throughout the Middle East, they have been perhaps most dramatic in Iran, where in 1979 the pro-Western regime was overthrown and replaced by the Islamic Republic. Another part of the Middle East, the smaller Persian Gulf states, have significantly progressed; where as late as 1965 only a few kilometers of surfaced road existed, now, for example, the United Arab Emirates is one of the most modern states of the developing world.

This book has striven to encourage thoughtful contemplation about the business environment of the Middle East and the course of globalization that is bound to affect the future of the region. Focusing on several key topics, the book has addressed trade relations among states, globalization issues, functional areas of human resource management, Islamic banking, marketing, and various issues connected with the internal business and economic dynamics of the region. Although this listing is by no means exhaustive, any identification of critical or relevant issues will surely include these. Surprisingly little indigenous discussion takes place regarding the future of the area. No regionwide consensus or outlook is emerging, and no Middle East perspective is crystallized regarding the future.

One must note that the Middle East is unique. Significant differences exist in social, economic, and business practices; the Middle East states are not as monolithic as some believe.

The contribution of this book has been to highlight and discuss some of these questions and to consider in as pragmatic a manner as possible the issues, practices, and problems that have been raised throughout its chapters. Included are questions on how government-MNE relations change as we move into the twenty-first century. How do these differ from past relations, becoming more cooperative or confrontational? What roles do institutions and political, social, and cultural environment play? What new lenses can scholars, policy makers, and practitioners use to understand the dynamics of the region? How must the international strategies of MNEs adjust in order to increase opportunities for citizens of this developing region, people who may not be fully prepared for the rigors of globalization, and to address issues raised by the darker side of globalization?

The Middle East is party to many of the changes taking place in the world. The success of the free market and the collapse of the communist model with its centralized economy are global phenomena that have influenced the region. Similarly, the globalization of business activities has had important ramifications for the region.

There is a feeling, however, that the Middle East has been slower to respond to these changes than the rest of the world, a perception especially evident with respect to issues connected to economic integration, privatization, and industrialization.

In the coming decade the Middle East will continue to be an important and prominent part of the world. Multinationals seeking to play an important role on the global stage will continue to show interest in the region. Global competition will ensure that strategic moves for increased presence will persist. The role the Middle East adopts for itself in this extraordinary new era will determine its national, regional, and corporate success or failure.

Selected Bibliography

Abu-Saad, I. (1998). "Individualism and Islamic Work Beliefs." *Journal of Cross-Cultural Psychology* 29:2.

Agra Europe, August 25, 1995.

Agra Europe, September 20, 1996.

Ahmed, S. A., and H. Donnan (Eds.) (1994). *Islam, Globalization and Post Modernity*. New York: Routledge.

Al-Aiban, K. M., and J. L. Pearce (1993). "The Influence of Values on Management Practices: A Test in Saudi Arabia and the United States." *International Studies of Management and Organization* 23: 3.

Al-Ashmawy, S. (1986). "Islamic Government." *Middle East Review*, Spring.

Ali, A. (1988). "A Cross-National Perspective of Managerial Work Value Systems." In *Advances in International Comparative Management*, Vol. 3. Greenwich, Conn.: JAI Press.

Ali, A., and R. Wahabi (1995). "Managerial Value Systems in Morocco: Management and Its Environment in the Arab World." *International Studies of Management and Organization* 25:3.

Alkhafaji, A. (1992). *The Gulf War: Implications for Global Business and Media*. Apollo, Pa.: Closson Press.

Amuzegar, J. (1993). *Iran's Economy*. London: IB Tauris.

Balaassa, B. (1961). *The Theory of Economic Integration*. Homewood, Ill.: Richard D. Irwin.

"Banking Sector Makes Progress toward Maturity" (1984). *Middle East Economic Digest (MEED)*, Special Report on Saudi Arabia, July.

Banks, S. (1986). "Cross-national Analysis of Advertising Expenditures: 1968–1979." *Journal of Advertising Research* 26:2, 11–24.

Barakat, H. (1993). *The Arab World: Society, Culture, and the State.* Berkeley: University of California Press.

Bertsch, G., and S. Elliot-Gower (1992). *Export Controls in Transition: Perspectives, Problems and Prospects.* Durham, N.C.: Duke University Press.

Bhaduri, A., and R. Skarstein (Eds.) (1997). *Economic Development and Agriculture Productivity.* Cheltenham, U.K.: Edward Elgar Publishing, Ltd.

Business America (1998). U.S. Department of Commerce. Washington, D.C.: International Trade Administration, February 10.

Chapra, M. U. (1986). *Towards a Just Monetary System.* Leicester, U.K.: Islamic Foundation.

Coats, W. L., and D. R. Khatkhate (1984). "Monetary Policy in Less Developed Countries: Main Issues." *Developing Economies*, no. 22.

Cooper, R. (1987). *Economic Policy in an Interdependent World.* Cambridge, Mass.: MIT Press.

Country Reports on Economic Policy and Trade Practices (1998). Washington, D.C.: U.S. Department of State, February 10.

Cummings, J. T., H. Askari, and A. Mustafa (1980). "Islam and Modern Economic Change." In John Esposito (Ed.), *Islam and Development.* Syracuse, NY: Syracuse University Press, pp. 25–49.

Czinkota, M. R., and M. Kotabe (1998) *Trends in International Business: Critical Perspectives.* Oxford: Blackwell.

"Egypt Lets Privatization into Oil Sector" (1998). *Privatization News*, June 15–21.

"Egypt Opens Insurance Sector to Foreign Investment" (1998). *Middle East Business Intelligence*, January 5.

Esposito, J. (Ed.) (1980). *Islam and Development.* Syracuse, NY: Syracuse University Press.

Foreign Trade Barriers (1993). U.S. Government publication, Washington, D.C.: Office of the United States Trade Representative.

Fox, S. (1985). *The Mirror Makers: A History of American Advertising and Its Creators.* New York: Vintage Books.

Frank, J. (1988). "Mis-communication across Cultures: The Case of Marketing in Indian English." *World Englishes*, 7:1, pp. 25–36.

"Free the Markets and Develop" (1983). *Euromoney*, May.

Gareau, F. (1986). "The Third World Revolution against First World Social Science." *International Journal of Comparative Sociology* 27.

"Gas Rich and Credit Hungry" (1996). *Euromoney*, May.

Gilly, M. (1988). "Sex Roles in Advertising: A Comparison of Television Advertisements in Australia, Mexico, and the United States." *Journal of Marketing* 52:2, 33–45.

Graham, E. F. (1991). *The Center of the Universe: The Geopolitics of Iran.* Boulder, Colo.: Westview Press.

Grant, R. (1996). *Contemporary Strategy Analysis.* Oxford: Blackwell.

Gumperz, J. (1982). *Discourse Strategies.* Cambridge: Cambridge University Press.

———. (1977). "Sociocultural Knowledge in Conversational Inference." In A. Saville-Troike (Ed.), *Linguistics and Anthropology.* Georgetown University Round Table on Languages and Linguistics, Washington, D.C.: Georgetown University Press, pp. 191–211.

Gumperz, J. and J. Cook-Gumperz (1981). "Ethnic Differences in Communicative Style." In Charles A. Ferguson and Shirley Brice Heath (Eds.), *Language in the USA.* Cambridge: Cambridge University Press, pp. 430–435.

Hamilton, M. (1998). "The Last Great Race for Oil Revenue?" *Washington Post*, April 26.

Hax, A., and S. Majluf (1996). *The Strategy Concept and Process: A Pragmatic Approach.* Englewood Cliffs, N.J.: Prentice Hall.

Hofstede, G. (1980). *Cultures Consequences: International Differences in Work-Related Values.* Beverly Hills, Calif.: Sage.

Huntington, S. (1997). *Clash of Civilizations: The Remaking of World Order.* New York: Touchstone.

International Financial Statistics (1997). Washington, D.C.: IMF.

International Monetary Fund (1994). *Direction of Trade Statistics Yearbook.* Washington, D.C.

Iran: Statistical Yearbook (1983). Tehran: Statistical Center of Iran.

Iran Times, February 12–April 15, 1998.

"Islamic Banking Gains Momentum, Expands Market and Competes with Conventional Banking in Arab States" (1998). *Middle East Executive Reports*, January.

"Islamic Funds Aim to Raise $1,500 Million" (1998). *Middle East Economic Digest (MEED)*, July 24.

Jackson, J. (1995). *The World Trading System.* Cambridge, Mass.: MIT Press.

Johnson, T. (1997). *Export/Import.* New York: Amacom.

Johnston, B. (1987). "Parataxis in Arabic: Modification as a Model for Persuasion." *Studies in Language* 11:1, 85–98.

———. (1983). "Presentation as Proof: The Language of Arabic Rhetoric." *Anthropological Linguistics* 25: 47–60.

Journal of Commerce (1994) 400: 28255 (June 27).

Kahf, M. (1981). "A Contribution to the Theory of Consumer Behavior in

Islamic Society." In K. Ahmad (Ed.), *Studies in Islamic Economics.* Jeddah, Saudi Arabia: International Center for Research on Islamic Economics; Leicester, U.K.: Islamic Foundation.

Kahn, A. (1985). "Resource Allocation in an Islamic Economy." *Islamic Quarterly* (Fourth Quarter).

Kaser, M. (1997). "Economic Transition in Six Central Asian Economies." *Central Asian Survey* 16:1.

Kashima, E. S., and Y. Kashima (1998). "Culture and Language." *Journal of Cross-Cultural Psychology*, May.

Kavoossi, M. (1988). "Islamic Interest Free Banking and Populist Islamic Ideology: Times of Transition." In R. Aggarawal and C. Crespy (Eds.), *Midwest Review of International Business Research.* Chicago: Academy of International Business.

Khatami, M. (1997). *Hope and Challenge: The Iranian President Speaks.* Binghamton, N.Y.: Binghamton University Press.

Khouri, R. L. (1987). "Islamic Banking: Knotting a New Network." *Armaco World*, September.

Kikeri, Sunita, et al. (1992). *Privatization: The Lessons of Experience.* Washington, D.C.: World Bank.

Koran, *Sura* [chapter] Tah, Ayat [verse] 25–34.

Kozan, M. K., and C. Ergin (1998). "Preference of Third Party Help in Conflict Management in the United States and Turkey: An Experimental Study." *Journal of Cross-Cultural Psychology* 29:4.

LeClair, M. (1997). *Regional Integration and Global Free Trade.* London: Avebury.

"Letting Go Speeds Up Expansion: Telecommunications Privatization" (1998). *MEED*, March 13.

Levin, R., and D. Renalt (1992). "A Sensitivity Analysis of Cross-Country Growth Regression." *American Economic Review* 82, 942–963.

Liberman, I. W. (1993). "Privatization: The Theme of the 1990s." *Columbia Journal of World Business* 28:1, 7–17.

Machlop, F. (1980). *Economic Integration: Worldwide, Regional, Sectoral.* London: Macmillan.

Madden, C. S., M. Cabvallero, and S. Masukubo (1986). "Analysis of Information Content in U.S. and Japanese Magazine Advertisements." *Journal of Advertising* 15:3, 38–45.

Maurice, S., and A. L. Winters (May 1998). "Dynamics and Politics in Regional Integration Arrangements: An Introduction." *World Bank Economic Review* 12:2.

McDonald, Kevin (1993). "Why Privatization Is Not Enough." *Harvard Business Review*, June.

MEED, September 5, 1997.

MEED, February 10, 1997.

Mehmet, O. (1990). *Islamic Identity and Development.* New York: Routledge.

Merriam, J. G., and A. J. Fluellen (1992). "Arab World Privatization: Key to Development." *Arab Studies Quarterly* 14:2 and 3 (Spring/Summer).

Ministry of Agriculture (1983–1997). *Agriculture Economic Report.* Tehran, Iran.

Mirsepassi, Nasser (1989). *Managing Human Resources and Labor Relations* (7th ed.). Tehran, Iran: Globe Publishing.

Molano, Walter (1997). *The Logic of Privatization: The Case of Telecommunications in the Southern Cone of Latin America.* Westport, Conn. Greenwood Press, p. 4.

Moody's International Manual (1996). New York: Vicki Pearthree Raeburn Publishers.

Moore, W. E. (1979). *World Development: Limits to Convergence.* New York: Elsevier.

Mottershaw, Elizabeth (1997). "Gulf Funds Primed for Privatization." *MEED*, June 13.

———. (1997). "Gulf Infrastructure Gets a Shake-Up." *MEED*, June 13.

Naqvi, Sayed Haider (1994). *Islam, Economics and Society.* London: Kegan Paul International.

"New Services, Same Old Rate Problems" (1993). *Middle East Economic Digest (MEED)*, March 26.

"OECD-Turkish Stability" (1998). *Turkish Times*, April 15.

Onkvisit, S., and J. Shaw (1987). "Standardized International Advertising: A Review and Critical Evaluation of the Theoretical and Empirical Evidence." *Columbia Journal of World Business*, Fall Issue, 43–55.

OPEC Bulletin (various issues).

"Overcoming Geography and Statism" (1998). *Institutional Investor*, July.

Pearl, D. (1998). "Rial Problems: Economic Woes Complicate Any Thaw with the U.S." *Wall Street Journal*, June 19.

Pomfret, R. (1997). "The Economic Cooperation Organization: Regional Forum or Irrelevant Talking Shop?" *Caspian Crossroads*, Spring.

Porter, M. (Ed.) (1986). *Competition in Global Industries.* Boston: Harvard Business School Press.

———. (1980). *Competitive Strategy.* New York: Free Press.

Posusney, Marsha (1992). "Labor as an Obstacle to Privatization." In I. Harik and O. Sullivan (Eds.), *Privatization and Liberalization in the Middle East.* Bloomington: Indiana University Press.

"Privatization and Growth of Financial Markets in the Gulf" (1995). *International Financial Law Review*, February.

"Privatization: Experience and Pitfalls" (1993). *Tadbir*, June.

Rajaee, F. (1983). *Islamic Values and World View*. Lanham, Md.: University Press of America.

"Reform Effort Needs to Shift Up a Gear" (1988). *MEED*, June 5.

Resnik, A., and B. Stern (1977). "An Analysis of Information Content in Television Advertisements." *Journal of Advertising* 41:1, 50–53.

Rice, M., and Z. Lu (1988). "A = 1F Content Analysis of Chinese Magazine Advertisements." *Journal of Advertising* 17:4, 41–48.

Richardson, D. (1993). *Sizing Up U.S. Export Disincentives*. Washington, D.C.: Institute for International Economics.

Root, F. (1994). *Entry Strategies for International Markets*. New York: Lexington.

Rostow, W. W. (1964). *The Stages of Economic Growth*. Cambridge: Cambridge University Press.

Roth, R. (1982). *International Marketing Communication*. Chicago: Crain.

"SAMA Listings Signals New Era for TAIC" (1984). *Middle East Economic Digest (MEED)*, Special Report on Saudi Arabia, July.

Sanaie, A. (1996). "Marketing in Islamic Countries: Iran's Case Study." *Journal of International Marketing and Marketing Research* 21:3.

Schott, J. (1988). *United States–Canada Free Trade: An Evaluation of the Agreement*. Washington, D.C.: Institute for International Economics.

Schott, J. J. (1994). *The Uruguay Round*. Washington, D.C.: Institute for International Economics.

Schuler, R., and N. Rogovsky (1998). "Understanding Compensation Practice Variations across Firms: The Impact of National Culture." *Journal of International Business Studies* 29:1.

Scollon, R., and S.B.K. Scollon (1981). *Narrative, Literacy and Face in Interethnic Communication*. Norwood, N.J.: Ablex.

Seznec, Jean-Françoise (1995). *Columbia Journal of World Business,* Fall.

Shackleton, V. J., and A. Ali (1990). "Work Related Values of Managers: A Test of Hofstede Model." *Journal of Cross-Cultural Psychology* 21.

Shane, S. (1988). "Language and Marketing in Japan." International *Journal of Advertising*, 155–161.

Sharifi, M. (1998). "The Export Supply Functions of Agriculture Products in Iran: An Estimation." *Iranian Journal of Trade Studies (IJTS) Quarterly* 2:6.

Shilling, N. A. (1983). *Marketing in the Arab World*. Dallas, Tex.: Inter-Crescent.

Sick, G. G., and L. Potter (Eds.) (1997). *The Persian Gulf at the Millennium*. New York: St. Martin's Press.

Smith, L. (Ed.) (1987). *Discourse across Cultures*. London: Prentice Hall.

Stern, B., D. Krugman, and A. Resnik (1981). "Magazine Advertising: An

Analysis of Its Information Content." *Journal of Advertising* 21:2, 39–44.

Stockel, A., and G. Banks (1990). *Western Trade Blocks.* Canberra, Australia: Center for International Economics.

Suriyamongkol, M. (1988). *Politics of Asian Economic Cooperation.* Oxford: Oxford University Press.

Talegani, S. M. (1983). *Islam and Ownership.* Tehran: Foundation of Islamic Thought.

Tarock, A., and A. Sewy (1997). "Iran's Policy in Central Asia." *Central Asian Survey* 16:2.

Temple, M. (1994). *Regional Economics.* London: St. Martin's Press.

Toyne, B., and D. Nigh (Eds.) (1997). *International Business: An Emerging Vision.* Columbia: University of South Carolina Press.

Vassilliou, G. (1983). *Marketing in the Middle East.* London: McCorquodele.

Viner, J. (1950). *The Customs Union Issue.* New York: Carnegie Endowment for International Peace.

Weekly, K. J., and R. Aggarwal (1987). *International Business: Operating in the Global Economy.* New York: Dryden Press.

"Western Banks Taking 1st Steps into Islam's 'No Interest' World" (1997). *American Banker* 162:20, January 30, p. 9.

Wind, Y. (1986). "The Myth of Globalization." *Journal of Consumer Marketing* 3, 23–26.

Withiam, G. (1994). *Cornell Hotel and Restaurant Administration Quarterly,* August.

World Development Report (WDR) (1995, 1997, 1999). World Bank. New York: Oxford University Press.

"Year of the Bull: Tehran's Stock Exchange" (1993). *Banker,* February.

Yildrim, T., A. Shmitz and W. H. Furtan (Eds.) (1998). *World Agriculture Trade.* Boulder, Colo.: Westview Press.

Zarrouk, J. E. (1992). "Intra-Arab Trade: Determinants and Prospects for Expansion." In El Najar Jaid (Ed.), *Foreign and Intra-Trade Politics of the Arab Countries.* Washington, D.C.: IMF.

Index